The Computer Buyer's Handbook

Alasdair Brodie

PUBLISHED BY NCC PUBLICATIONS

British Library Cataloguing in Publication Data

Brodie, Alasdair
The computer buyer's handbook
1. Computer systems – Buyers' guides
I. Title
004'.029'4

ISBN 0-85012-696-7

First published in 1988 by:

NCC Publications, The National Computing Centre Limited, Oxford Road, Manchester M1 7ED, England.

Typeset in 11pt Times Roman by H&H Graphics, 2 Duke Street, Blackburn; and printed by Hobbs the Printers of Southampton.

ISBN 0-85012-696-7

Contents

Introduction
Into the Maze

For the inexperienced purchaser, trying to buy the right computer for your business is like walking into a maze. If there was only one exit it wouldn't be so bad, but you soon learn that nothing in the computer world is that simple. This maze has multiple exits. Not one of them is exactly correct, and most are false exits, leading only to more problems.

Even if you've successfully negotiated this maze before, when it's time to buy a new system most of the routes you followed in the past will have changed. Even experts sometimes get lost in this maze.

The biggest problem for buyers is lack of knowledge. It isn't just a case of knowing which computers are 'good' and which aren't. These days most computers are 'good'. It isn't even knowing which programs are right for your business, although that is a definite step nearer the answer. It is more a case of understanding the whole buying-selling-recommending process that occurs whenever you enter the maze.

There are almost certainly a number of sound and trustworthy companies out there that are able to supply the correct system for your needs. The problem – and it can seem insurmountable at times – is to find them. Where do you start to look? How do you even know when you've found a reputable company? And one particular question follows on from these – where do you turn to for advice?

The aim of this book is to answer questions like these. Reading this book will not guarantee that you get the perfect computer system (it probably doesn't exist), but it should assist you in getting much closer to the optimum solution for your business.

The first thing to learn is that there aren't any easy short-cuts. Getting the right system will take some work, but it should be amply repaid. A well selected computer system will pay for itself and make money for your business. This doesn't mean that every business, or every department, needs a computer. How do you know? The last section of this book suggests ways to answer this often tricky question.

But to begin at the beginning, Part 1 of this book examines the various computer sales organisations in the UK marketplace. Each has its own strengths and weaknesses, and this book seeks to point these out. The divisions in the book have been set up mainly for the sake of clarity, but should not be taken as mutually exclusive or fixed. Nothing is ever simple in the computer world.

Part 2 delves into the complex world of consultancy companies. This is one of the most difficult areas in the computer maze. Finding a consultancy company which actually knows what it's talking about, or is as impartial as it's supposed to be is a lot more difficult than you might think. This makes life difficult for businesses. If you don't have the time or the knowledge to choose your own system, the obvious thing to do is to turn to a consultant. But many 'consultancies' are sales organisations in disguise (to complicate things further, this is sometimes a good thing), and many 'real' consultancies lack the knowledge to give proper assistance. It is often harder to choose a good consultant than it is to choose a computer supplier.

However, this is not to say that there aren't any good consultancies out there. Many are in fact excellent. The trick, of course, is to know how to find them. This book give an overview of this sector, and gives some pointers that makes the selection process easier.

Part 3 is the self-help section. Before approaching sales or consultancy organisations it is often very useful to have done some groundwork yourself. But where to start? This section explores the various ways open to computer buyers to increase their knowledge of computing on their own, without using sales organisations or consultancies.

As everyone in business is busy, and has limited time to concentrate on learning about computers, the focus of Part 3 is on the quick and easy ways to learn more. After all, a computer is just a business tool. You don't have to know how a tool works in order to use it. But understanding the basics is always useful, especially when facing 'experts'.

This overview may seem to paint a rather gloomy picture of the computer maze. But after reading a book such as this, and checking out the other information sources available, things will become much clearer. There are many good systems, and many excellent computer suppliers, but very few simple solutions. The small amount of effort required to learn, plus the advantage of knowing what goes on inside the maze, should greatly assist you in finding the right system. And this effort will reward you with a more efficient and consequently a more profitable business.

The point to keep in mind is that while understanding how a computer works is useful, understanding how to buy the correct one will have far greater benefits. Knowing just what goes on in the computer maze is the key, and this book should be a major step in that direction.

* * *

There are some important points that readers of this book should note. Firstly it should be made clear that it is aimed at buyers of personal computers, multi-user systems, and small minicomputers. Although many of the points raised in the book are also of use to prospective purchasers of larger systems, most of the organisations named in these pages are active at the smaller systems end of the market. And some of the conclusions reached do *not* apply to the large systems marketplace.

Secondly, it should be made very clear that the companies named in the book are merely a cross-section of those plying their wares in the maze – it is not even a list of all the major names in the computer world. THIS IS *NOT* A DIRECTORY OF COMPUTER SUPPLIERS AND CONSULTANCY ORGANISATIONS. Anyone seeking such a directory should consult Chapter 10. The reason for 'naming names' is to give you an idea of the sort of companies that are out there, and of the various types of systems and services that are on offer. It may well be that none of the organisations named can supply the solution that's right for you, and this 'company overview' should be treated as a starting point in your search for the best supplier for your needs. (For example, it is impossible in a book such as this to give a listing of local computer dealers – and they may often be your best choice of supplier. You will have to seek that information elsewhere.)

Finally, a message to these suppliers and consultants: if you feel left out, or hard done by, please write to the author (care of the NCC). Your comments will help to keep potential new editions of this book fully up-to-date.

Part 1

Computer Sales Organisations

1 Local Computer Dealers

A Little Knowledge can be Dangerous

GENERAL

Local dealers encapsulate a large proportion of what is good and bad in computer supply organisations in general. On the one hand they can often provide an excellent service; on the other the lack of knowledge and staff in some of the smaller dealers can be a serious drawback. Like many other areas of computing, the decision whether or not to use a local dealer is not a simple one. The main consideration is often the size of computer installation that you are considering.

It should be recognised, however, that the vast majority of computer suppliers *are* local dealers, and that this is the type of supplier that you are most likely to encounter. The better local computer dealers are tending towards specialisation as a means of efficiently harnessing their sometimes limited resources, and this is of benefit to prospective buyers. This trend towards specialisation means that there is a substantial degree of overlap between the strengths and weaknesses of the sort of company discussed in this chapter and those examined in Chapter 3 (Specialist Computer Dealers) and Chapter 7 (Specialist Computer Consultants).

THE BENEFITS

A major benefit to be gained from buying from local dealers is the personal service they can provide. If you are buying for a large company, you may be the dealer's biggest customer and so, as near as is ever possible, you can be guaranteed the best service that dealer can provide. Often this service makes itself felt in the speed of response. Bigger suppliers usually have a number of customers to look after, and you may not be top of the list. With a local dealer, often located very near your offices, it is usually possible to have someone on your site in a matter of minutes, rather than hours (or days in some of the worst cases).

Local dealers, due to time and cost pressures, are very often experts in a particular range of hardware and software. Indeed, if this is so it is usually a sign of astute management. These dealers have limited resources and concentrating them on one or two particular products or markets can bring great rewards. Interestingly some dealers are small out of choice and temperament. They are often very small outfits with less than five members of staff, and owned by one person. The owner is temperamentally unsuited to working in large organisations and instead has created a superb and knowledgeable small company, dedicated to marketing quality products backed up by an excellent service.

Another consideration is the fact that the dealers *are* local. This can mean that they know the area, and more importantly, know about your business. This can save a great deal of time normally spent on educating suppliers about your requirements and budget constraints. It is also the policy of some local authorities to purchase from local dealers whenever possible to keep trade and employment in the authorities' designated area. Indeed for companies whose operations are situated in more rural areas buying from a local dealer may be the only sensible option.

So, the main benefits of buying from local computer dealers are:

- the potential quality of service;
- you may be one of their biggest customers – and get a guaranteed quick response;
- the best of the dealers will build up a specialist knowledge of a limited range of products or markets (this topic is dealt with in more detail in Chapters 3 and 7);
- the dealers can often have a good understanding of the area, or of your particular needs.

THE DRAWBACKS

The major drawback is the one that gave this chapter its subheading: some local computer dealers can often have a disturbing lack of knowledge about what they're selling. And the little they do know can do more harm than good. (Luckily this seems to apply to a decreasing number of dealers.)

In the worst case, businesses find out about this lack of know-how when it's far too late. For instance, the first installation from a local dealer may be a simple one and they can handle it very well. But then you want something more complicated. 'No problem' says the dealer, and then proceeds to make a complete hash of it. And as many businesses have found out to their cost, a badly installed or just plain incorrect system for the task can cost a company substantially more than the expense of finding a true professional supplier in the first place.

This potential lack of knowledge has two main sources. The first, and most dangerous, is that some of the smaller local dealers are plainly incompetent. This is why they are, and always will be, small and local. But a persuasive sales pitch can hide the inadequacies, and drag companies into the muddy byways of the computer maze. Fortunately this seems to be happening less often than in the early days of computing as business personnel have steadily increased their knowledge of what computers can and can't do. Many large companies are now more knowledgeable than some suppliers.

The second source of the problem is one facing many different companies in various market sectors: a lack of cash. The smaller local dealers often genuinely want to be more knowledgeable and to provide a superior service to their customers. But the computer maze is becoming more complex, not less so. It takes time and money to gather all the necessary information to provide the sort of service that clued-up businesses demand, and this time and money may just not be available.

A problem directly linked to this is the difficulty small companies (of any sort) have in finding and holding on to quality professional staff. In the fast moving and complicated electronic world, having staff that have a totally professional outlook, are able to assimilate new ideas, and can then effectively implement these ideas on a practical level is almost becoming a prerequisite. The smaller local dealers can have difficulties in offering the sort of salaries or career paths that larger companies can offer.

This leads directly into another major problem: a general shortage of staff. This can often have a devastating effect on the quality of service smaller dealers can provide. It is too often the case that small dealers rely very heavily on one or two key members of staff to handle most of their workload. If these people then depart (usually to larger companies) then the dealer can be left in the very awkward position of having customers demanding support, and not having anyone capable of giving this support. And as quality people are in short supply, it can be quite some time before a proper replacement is found.

Sometimes it is a dealer's success that is to blame. A small dealer can be growing rapidly, and bringing in more and more customers. This puts a great strain on the available resources. Judging when to employ more staff, and then locating the right people, is a very delicate process. If it is handled incorrectly then it is the existing customers who suffer.

Similarly, if it is the customer's business that is growing rapidly, the dealer may not be able to keep up the level of support required. If the dealer pulls in extra people just for this one contract, it can be financially catastrophic if that contract is then lost. Judging when to bring in extra staff is often the skill that separates the successes from the failures.

A problem coupled with this lack of staff is that local dealers are just that: local. They tend to have only a few offices, sometimes as many as five, all in a fairly tight geographical area. This means that if a large corporation with sites all over the country wants supply and local support from a single source then these types of companies don't even get considered.

However a number of the larger companies allow their local offices a fair degree of independent control over computer purchase decisions, and in these cases local dealers can be included on purchasing shortlists. Some national companies that do have central control of purchasing do buy from local companies as a matter of policy, looking for some of the benefits outlined above. But on the whole it is seldom that a local dealer lands a major contract from a large corporation (this mainly applies to hardware installations; specialist software may not be available from any other source).

The last major drawback of buying from a local dealer is the question of financial security, or more correctly, financial *in*security. Of course, this is not just a problem with local dealers. Over the last few troubled years a number of larger national suppliers such as Interface plc and First Computer have folded. But when one of the bigger suppliers collapses there is sometimes another company willing to step in and pick up some of the pieces, ie their former competitors want the ex-company's customers (in computer jargon: user-base). This is not always the case, and it is seldom a smooth transition when it does occur, but at least it holds out the prospect of some continuity of supply.

However things are more complicated at the smaller end. For a start, smaller dealers go out of business at a greater rate than do the larger ones. Some of the more alarmist press comments suggest that IBM could lose as many as 40% of its dealers over 1987/1988. (This isn't quite as bad as it looks, as in this period new dealers will also emerge.) Secondly, there is far less chance of another company stepping in to take over the existing customers. There are usually too few of them, buying too little equipment to make it worthwhile. This means that in most cases when a small dealer folds (or drops the computer side of its business due to lack of profits) the existing customers get left in the lurch. If this happens just as a company is in the process of installing a new system, it can be a very painful and costly experience.

In many ways companies have brought this situation on themselves by demanding ever increasing discounts on equipment purchases. There is a shortage of the sort of quality staff required and it costs a lot of money to secure their services. In addition, the retail cost of computer systems has decreased markedly, and dealers' profit margins have dropped with it. As long as businesses demand greater and greater discounts they will be running an ever increasing risk of forcing their suppliers to go broke. In the long run this situation benefits no one.

However it is not all gloom and doom. The shakeout in the

market has had one major advantage – the 'fly-by-nights' are finding it increasingly difficult to stay in business. These are small local dealers who give all dealers a bad name. They start up, cause havoc for a few months, go out of business, then start up again in a few months' time under a new name. As profit margins have decreased this type of rip-off operation has found the rewards no longer to their liking. Unfortunately it probably means that they've gone off to plague businesses in another sector of the market.

In summary, the main drawbacks to buying from a small local computer dealer are:

— a (sometimes dangerous) lack of knowledge among the smaller dealers;

— the lack of (quality) staff to handle large or complex installations;

— too few locations for larger corporations wanting hardware installations in multiple sites;

— possible financial insecurity.

CONCLUSION

Most of the drawbacks outlined above apply to the *smaller* local dealer – many local dealers have large and substantial operations and are less prone to these drawbacks. However the pressures outlined above are a major reason for the trend towards specialisation. Local computer dealers that can offer a range of specialist skills are very often the best choice of supplier for your computer system.

Have a look at Chapters 3 and 7 for a further analysis of specialist computer suppliers.

2 National/Substantial Computer Dealers

Beware of Boxshifters

GENERAL

National/substantial computer dealers are the major players in the computer supply world, or at least they're the companies with the most grandiose claims. The aim of this group is to be major suppliers to the high volume corporate market – the plc's of this world. But they are all willing, to a greater or lesser degree, to sell to smaller companies and first-time users. At the PC level they can be subdivided into three groups:

— dealerships;

— mail order outlets;

— high street shops.

Each of these groups has very different philosophies about how and what to sell, and this chapter examines their competing strengths and weaknesses.

COMPUTER DEALERSHIPS

By the middle of 1987, the maturing process in the computer world had forced a number of closures and mergers among computer dealerships. Interface plc folded, and their sales force were taken on by MBS (who themselves had nearly gone bankrupt a few months earler). First Computer then disappeared, and the acquisitive MBS then took over Combro, a major supplier of PCs to the corporates. Many other smaller dealers either disappeared altogether, or were taken over by their larger competitors (Computacenter's takeover of London-based Merchant Systems being an example). The following major companies still have nationwide operations:

- MBS;
- Computacenter;
- Computerland;
- Specialist Computer Centres (SCC).

As you can see, this is a very small list. However in the substantial (but not national) category fall companies such as P & P (formerly a distributor of PC products, now engaged in direct sales to corporates as well); Personal Computers (strong in the London area); Centre-File (owned by the NatWest Bank); and the Businessland operation in the south (formerly the Granada Business Centres). There are a number of suppliers of larger systems who also have national outlets (such as the Fraser Williams Group), but they are not the main focus of this book.

As these national/substantial computer dealers account for a very significant proportion of the systems sold in the UK, it is worth examining the reasons why they have reached this position. Are they the right sort of companies for inexperienced buyers to approach? And what are the (always present) drawbacks to their way of working?

THE BENEFITS

One of the common claims made by the major computer dealers is that they have a greater store of knowledge and expertise than do the smaller dealers. This is probably true in some limited areas, but not in all. Their real strength is their ability to meet the demands of the corporate marketplace. One of these factors is the sheer scale of their operations. Large companies like to buy from large companies, and national operations like to buy from national suppliers. The second important factor is the prices they are willing to sell at. With large orders from customers, plus larger discounts from their suppliers the major dealers can often go to what seems like ridiculous lengths to buy business. The business philosophy of successful suppliers to the corporates, such as P & P Micro and

Combro (now part of MBS) seems to be "We will match or beat the discounts offered by our competitors".

The claim of greater knowledge and expertise than smaller dealers is seldom true (often the reverse is the case). What *is* really important is the scale of the support operations that companies like MBS, Computacenter and SCC can bring to bear on major installations. For an important client they can pull in key staff from a number of locations and form a highly professional-looking team to handle the installation. Their claims to greater expertise are also related to this size factor. Economies of scale make it possible for them to form specialist divisions covering areas such as communications, networking and multi-user systems; and these divisions alone can have more staff than the entire complement at a smaller dealer.

There is also the administrative and storage elements to consider. A company has to have a large and efficient warehousing facility in order to cope with rapid deliveries of large orders (although there are probably a lot of customers who have found that this claim is not always proved correct). It takes a great deal of money, good lines of credit, and a large and efficient sales force to justify the holding of vast quantities of stock. Many smaller dealers are not capable of handling very large orders of equipment, although it should be remembered that these major dealers were once small dealers themselves that managed to control very rapid growth without bankrupting themselves in the process.

In theory these large organisations should be more financially secure than their smaller brethren, but the disappearance of over five major dealers in 1987 (by either financial collapse or takeover) somewhat undermines this potential benefit. Large dealers caught in a price war can end up with huge quantitities of stock that they are unable to shift, and this can topple them even faster than smaller dealers with manageable stockholdings. For example UBS's computer sales organisation pulled out of the market saying that they had found it impossible to make a profit, despite a fairly large turnover. MBS, the largest supplier in the PC market, nearly went bust in the middle of a price war in 1985, and were only saved by a management buy-in. However there are signs that at the national / substantial dealer end of the market things are beginning to settle down again as the maturing process continues.

The major dealers also tend to be less biased towards one or two manufacturers as they can cope with selling a number of product lines. This improves the choice available to potential customers, but it sometimes puts a strain on the support operation which is required to look after this diversity of computer equipment. In the corporate market this choice is not as vital, as companies tend to be heavily biased towards IBM products. For smaller customers this choice is important as they are less blinkered in their approach to buying computers.

The whole question of price levels and discounts is one that continues to plague the computer supply industry, especially at the PC level. Calling a company 'boxshifters' used to be exclusively a term of abuse, but as many corporates now have highly professional internal support departments, boxshifting at high discounts with little or no support backup is just what they want. The appearance of Amstrads and IBM PS/2s in high street shops such as Dixons has increased the 'commoditisation' of personal computers, and this coupled with the increasing skill levels of users helped organisations such as P & P and Combro along the road to success. Many of the major suppliers are trying to escape from the 'commodity market' by increasing their sales of up-market systems (such as multi-user systems and small minicomputers) and by offering more value-added services (eg service and support contracts; cabling; communications expertise, etc) to lift their profit levels once more. This change in the public's perception of the personal computer (from a symbol of high technology to just another commodity) is just one of the signs of a maturing market.

The benefits of buying from national/substantial computer dealers are:

- excellent support for large projects;
- they sometimes have a high degree of expertise, often via specialist divisions;
- they should (in theory) be more financially secure than smaller dealers;
- large volume sales and large volume purchase agreements allow them to sell at deep discounts (this is a service often

demanded by customers, but it is not always as beneficial as you might think – see 'Drawbacks' below).

THE DRAWBACKS

The 'beware of boxshifters' warning at the start of this chapter is aimed at users who require a fairly high degree of support when they purchase a computer system. A number of companies have been caught out in the past by negotiating what they thought were excellent discount levels, only to find that this discount carried a hidden price – when they asked for support they got little or no response. This, it has to be said, is hardly surprising. What is surprising is that many companies were under the impression that they could secure big discounts and still get top-quality support without bankrupting their suppliers. A top-quality support operation costs a lot of money, and many of the suppliers who attempted this high discount/top-quality support trick did indeed go out of business.

There will, however, always be companies who demand exactly this sort of purchase agreement. In cases where good support is essential, you should be wary of suppliers who claim to offer an all-singing, all-dancing support operation at massive discounts. Accepting a lower discount initially in return for better support may well prove to be better value for money in the longer term.

The support operations of the major suppliers can often be highly centralised, so if you are a small customer in a remote location your chances of receiving the best support possible from a large supplier is probably also remote. On the whole smaller customers with low purchase volumes are less important to these large operations. To shift their massive stock holdings they need massive orders, so a company that is ordering ten PCs a month is clearly going to be higher up their list of priorities than a company which orders two or three machines a year. And if one of these three machines breaks down at the same time as a 10-station network at the bigger customer, guess which site the maintenance engineer will visit first! However that one PC may be more vital to the smaller company's business than the network is to the larger customer. This is not to say that these major suppliers don't endeavour to offer the same level of support to all their customers, large or small. It is just a fact of life that commercial logic often intrudes.

The necessary scale of the big suppliers' operations also means that they are not geared to support the needs of small volume specialist markets. Their support operations tend towards the needs of the mass market, so if your requirements are decidedly non-standard you will almost certainly be better off going to a smaller dealer who can offer a higher level of support, or to a specialist dealer. These other dealers can often offer something that is distinctly lacking from larger operations – a higher degree of personal contact at director level. With a major supplier the highest level executive you are likely to meet (unless it is a very important large order) is the local branch manager, who is often quite a small cog in the large supplier machine. With smaller dealers and specialist suppliers you can often find yourself dealing directly with one of the owners of the business. This gives you a far greater insight into the business philosophy of the supplier, and also, if things go wrong, a direct line into someone with the authority to put things right in a short space of time.

These are the main drawbacks to buying from national/substantial computer dealers:

- boxshifting operations: good prices but a lack of often vital support;
- the support expertise available may be centralised and not readily available at remote locations;
- the whole thrust of the major suppliers is towards large volume generalist business, so if your requirements are non-standard you'll probably have to look elsewhere;
- there can be a lack of personal contact at higher executive levels;
- for commercial reasons smaller customers are less important to these suppliers than are large customers.

CONCLUSION

The third point of the drawback list (above) could also be used as a summary for this Conclusion. National/substantial computer dealers have to shift large volumes of equipment to sustain their bulk. To do this they must sell in the generalist marketplace. For this reason all of the successful operations are geared up to support large projects and large installations, and can offer the discount levels required to obtain this business.

Smaller businesses with low volume purchases are less important to them, and smaller businesses with specialist requirements are just not catered for in most instances. So if you are a smaller business with specialist requirements you'll probably be better approaching either local or specialist computer dealers. But for larger organisations with high volume PC purchases, this is the type of organisation that is geared to meet your needs (but remember that some of your departments may have specialist needs – they'd be better going to the same dealers as smaller businesses).

MAIL ORDER OUTLETS

Mail order outlets range from companies who place 'build your own computer' adverts in the PC press, to the relatively sophisticated boxshifting operations of organisations such as Mayfair Micros. Organisations of this sort are not of much use to your average computer buyer. They are aimed at either individual computer enthusiasts, or at large corporations with their own sophisticated PC support departments.

The larger mail order outlets can often supply machines at rock-bottom prices, but for that you will receive a few boxes and absolutely nothing else – from the day you've placed the order you are on your own. A few enterprising companies without existing PC support operations may be able to cope with this, but most companies need assistance in choosing the best system in the first place, and then need more assistance to get the best return from that system.

CONCLUSION

The moral is: mail order outlets are for the braver and more adventurous among us. It is no accident that these operations have not captured a larger market share despite their low prices. Even large corporations with long established PC support departments often find themselves in need of expert assistance when installing new systems – and they usually find that paying for this assistance proves to be more cost effective.

HIGH STREET SHOPS

For most of the high street retailers, starting to sell home computers was a big step. And very few of them have ever gone any further, scared off by the implications of selling true business systems. The major exception in this sector is Dixons who've put a fairly massive effort behind the retailing of systems for small businesses. Dixons are the true pioneers of the 'commodity' selling approach to business computers.

Dixons started off by selling Sanyo microcomputers which ran packages such as WordStar. They then added Amstrad micros to their range, and they are now Amstrad's biggest retailer. But their real breakthrough into business systems came when they signed a deal with IBM which enabled them to sell IBM's new PS/2 Model 30 systems, along with IBM's peripherals, and IBM-badged software such as the Solo accounting package and the Displaywrite word-processing package. The Sanyo and Amstrad micros are perfectly capable of running business software, but they were not perceived to be in the same league as IBM. The deal with IBM allows Dixons to claim to be a true business systems supplier (although their present offerings are so restricted as to make this statement only partially true).

To be successful in this market, Dixons have found that they've had to offer some of the services that ordinary computer dealers offer – hardware maintenance contracts (through a sub-contractor) and some form of computer support. It's this second point that causes most potential purchasers to be wary: just how good is the support from Dixons? Dixons have tried to make it easier on themselves by restricting their software offerings to two or three IBM products. They have some staff trained up to a higher level, but they still rely on IBM-backed telephone support operations in many cases. And when it comes to accounting systems such as Solo, one on-site visit by an expert can be worth a dozen telephone calls.

CONCLUSION

Dixons have been in this market for a relatively short period of time, so it is probably too early to judge whether their new venture will be a success. If saving some money on the purchase price of a computer system is a primary consideration, then you should perhaps have a look at what Dixons have to offer. For most other businesses probably the best advice is to wait and see whether Dixons' experiment works or not.

3 Specialist Computer Dealers

One-Way Streets?

GENERAL

The word 'specialist', like the word 'consultant', is heavily overworked in the computer world. Nearly every dealer in existence claims to be a specialist in at least one aspect of IT. A great number of specialist computer dealers also claim to be consultants, and there is a substantial degree of overlap between this chapter and Chapter 7 (Specialist Computer Consultancies). You would perhaps expect the word 'consultancy' to describe an organisation whose role is to give unbiased advice on computing requirements. But things are not that simple in the computer maze.

A large number of computer sales organisations also describe themselves as consultants, and indeed can give advice and recommendations, but these are heavily biased towards their own products and services. Even freelance programmers and system analysts describe themselves as consultants these days.

Likewise, there are very few companies who can live up to the label of 'specialist'. You should also be aware that the term specialist in no way implies a lack of bias. Most specialists specialise in selling their own products and services.

So what does constitute a specialist computer dealer? In its most general sense it refers to a dealer who has chosen to specialise in one or two areas of the market. More specifically it refers to a dealer who sells to one or two vertical markets. This is a marketing term which usually designates a group of companies in one particular sector of the market (such as accountants) or a group of users with similar requirements (such as manufacturing companies who would benefit from computer-aided engineering). Examples are Miles 33 who supply systems to solicitors, and Till Computer Systems who sell point-of-sale retail systems.

It also describes software houses that have developed a software package for a specific market, who then sell hardware as well as a means to selling their own software. An example is Practical Technology in Glasgow, who have developed the Daxcad computer-aided design package and who also sell a range of hardware to run their system. Similarly, hardware manufacturers often add software to their systems to enable them to supply a complete solution, eg Calcomp who also sell computer-aided design systems – from plotters to full CAD workstation systems.

Possibly the nearest example of a true specialist computer dealer is to be found in the organisations which supply fully integrated hardware and software systems (hardware and software which they have usually developed themselves) to just one vertical market. The burgeoning financial services sector provides a number of examples of this type of company, eg NMW Computers (specialising in broker systems); ACS (money markets and international banking); ACT Financial Systems, a subsidiary of Apricot plc (investment management and banking sysems); and Misys (broker systems).

There are very few specialist dealers with nationwide operations. Most of them are local operations selling to local companies, or selling nationwide from a local base. Those that do sell nationally often do so in a link up with another local dealer or, for those who are better organised, through a chain of appointed subdealers. The reason for this is quite simple: specialist dealers do not sell the large quantities required to justify nationwide offices. Even plc-sized operations like Miles 33, NMW and Misys do not stretch to nationwide offices.

So what are the benefits and drawbacks of buying from specialist computer dealers?

THE BENEFITS

To truly earn the title of 'specialist' these dealers should have in-depth specialist knowledge of the markets and equipment they are dealing with. But as outlined above, very few of the companies that claim to be specialist are actually worthy of the description. Specialist computer dealers very often produce their own hardware and software, and should have a depth of knowledge on the equipment and the requirements of one or two market sectors. If they do not produce their own hardware or software, then they should have a substantial degree of expertise in the needs of a particular vertical market, and then seek out and sell products which meet these needs. Either way, they should have 'specialist' knowledge, ie far greater knowledge or expertise than you would expect to find from an average generalist computer dealer.

A good method of finding out about whether a dealer actually lives up to these claims is to ask for a list of installations and reference sites. Reputable specialist dealers will have no problem in providing such a list, and they will be happy to let you speak to their existing customers. New dealers may not be able to provide a large list – but check that they are honest about being fresh to the market, and have a look at their products to see if they meet your requirements. But beware of dealers who give evasive answers, and cannot provide you with a list despite protestations that such a thing actually exists. On the other hand, do not always accept that this list of users is entirely accurate – some dealers will, for obvious reasons, not include their disasters on the list. Your own assessment of the people you are talking to must be the final judgement.

If the dealers you are talking to are truly specialist, then they should be able to offer a greater degree of expert support than can a general market dealer. Their knowledge of your business should mean that, unlike other suppliers, they do not have to learn about your business needs before they get on with the installation and training and subsequent support. This should mean that the system you purchase is up and running and making you money in a shorter timespan than would otherwise be the case.

This 'timespan' aspect is one of the main benefits to using a specialist computer dealer. Generalist dealers may well be capable of supplying and installing a suitable system, but it may take them substantially longer to understand your requirements and to get the system working to your satisfaction, especially if some bespoke programming is required. A specialist dealer should start from a position of greater knowledge of your needs, and the system they offer should require a minimum of modification. If this is not the case, then perhaps you should question their claim to be a 'specialist'.

A final, somewhat intangible, benefit to be gained from buying from a specialist dealer is that it is possible that they will have a more caring attitude towards their customers. This is much more likely to be true if they are a small company whose staff have actually been involved in the gestation and production of the final product they offer to the market. Anyone who is partly responsible for the creation of a product is much more likely to have a personal vested interest in making sure that that product works well and meets the requirements of the users. Therefore it can be worth finding out if the person you are in contact with has had any direct involvement in the development process of the product you are considering.

These are the main benefits of buying from a specialist computer dealer:

- they should have in-depth knowledge of the products they offer and of the needs of your market sector;
- they will be capable of giving expert support and guidance in selection and implementation of a computer system;
- their expert knowledge should substantially reduce the amount of time you spend in selecting a system, and having this system installed and working;
- smaller companies whose staff have been involved in the creation of the system on offer may well have a more caring attitude towards their customers, and be keener to see that the system works to your full satisfaction.

THE DRAWBACKS

As already suggested, the term 'specialist' is open to abuse. There are a substantial number of companies who claim to be specialists but are nothing of the sort. Be especially wary of suppliers who claim to be specialists but who can also supply you with 'everything and anything'. This sort of outfit treats the term specialist merely as a marketing ploy, and their claims of special knowledge generally lack any substance.

Specialist dealers who are true to the term can often have a disturbing lack of knowledge of other systems you may be considering – a sort of 'one way street' approach to computing. This can mean that you may have to use a number of suppliers to get the computer systems you want, not always a satisfactory solution, either from an accounting, or a 'who's to blame' viewpoint. If the specialist dealers you are talking to are honest about their strengths and weaknesses they will inform you when you step outside their area of specialisation. But again, be wary of specialists who start to offer you advice on other systems – you may have passed from sound specialist advice to the passing on of general market rumours.

Specialist dealers who confine themselves to a very narrow area of the market may achieve a commendably high level of knowledge of this market sector, but they also leave themselves more open to possible market changes, whether it be the whims of fashion or from increased competition. A change in the hardware policy of the manufacturer's system they have chosen to use, or the sudden appearance of a competitor with a vastly improved product, can leave them, and by extension your company, high and dry. If you have committed your company to using the fully bespoke software of a specialist supplier and that supplier then goes out of business you can be left with a very expensive mess to clean up. That is why it is usually essential to check not only if the system is suitable, but also to establish how many other installations the company has achieved (there is a certain degree of safety in numbers) and whether they have good prospects for survival in what can be a very competitive area of the market.

The final major drawback to consider is that all specialist dealers will be heavily biased towards their own products. *All* dealers are biased towards their own products but at least some of the general market dealers will be able to offer you some degree of choice from their product range. Specialist dealers may have only one or two different systems to offer, and this reduced choice can lead to problems. If your company itself is in a very specialist market sector then you may have no choice but to risk it, but it may well be worth a couple of extra months of search to see if your choice can be widened. The key to extending your choice is knowing where to look, which is a subject covered in the third part of this book.

The drawbacks to buying from specialist computer dealers are:

— a lot of dealers use the term 'specialist' purely as a marketing ploy;

— specialist dealers can lead you up one way streets – a change of direction or choice is not permitted;

— specialist dealers can be more prone to the winds of change, and can leave you with a large number of problems if they go broke;

— they tend to be even more biased than their general market counterparts.

CONCLUSION

Due to ever increasing competitive and cost pressures in the general computer marketplace, there have been an increasing number of dealers moving towards some form of specialisation as a way of escaping from ever decreasing profits. In some people's eyes this is a sad departure from the heady pioneering spirit in the early days of the PC world. But as these pioneers often took some of their customers with them as they went down to a dusty death, very few users rue the passing of this period. The move towards specialisation is a healthy sign of a maturing market, and this maturity benefits both the better dealers and their customers.

Despite the abuse of the term 'specialist', there is a substantial number of genuinely skilled specialist dealers in the marketplace, and their continuing success proves that their skills are being well received by computer users. True specialist knowledge of computers *and* business requirements is still quite rare in the computer world – so dealers that can offer this combination are to be welcomed. As long as you take steps to establish that you are dealing with *real* specialists, as opposed to 'marketing ploy' specialists, then these dealers can often be the best choice of suppliers for computer systems.

4 Computer Manufacturers

The Devil You Know . . .

GENERAL

People sometimes say "I buy direct from the manufacturer. Better the devil you know than the devil you don't". This approach has its attractions. Many computer manufacturers are household names, 'blue chip' companies with sound reputations, so it appears sensible to cut out the middleman, the dealer.

If it is that easy, then why are there so many successful and prosperous computer dealers? The answer is obvious: it isn't that easy. However easy the answer may be, the reasons are somewhat more complicated (as always in the maze). For a start, some manufacturers, such as Compaq, Amstrad and Altos, do not sell direct to end-users, preferring to use dealer channels. This is much more prevalent among smaller manufacturers at the microcomputer end of the market. So if you want their machines, you have no choice, you'll have to go to a dealer.

Historically minicomputer and mainframe manufacturers have tended to have direct sales forces, but even this is changing. The giant of them all, IBM, is considering pushing larger systems through their dealer channels. This is due to a general trend towards specialisation throughout the computer industry. It follows the logical argument that manufacturers are best at manufacturing, and sales organisations, the dealers, are best at selling and supporting. It is this question of support that is often the deciding factor that causes a manufacturer to shun direct sales. Selling is fine, but every system, once sold, requires support. As pointed out in Chapter 1, the world of computers is becoming more complex, not less so;

therefore to take on a support operation requires a substantial and continuing financial investment.

The old argument put forward by minicomputer manufacturers was that there were no dealers capable of supporting their products, so they had to do it themselves. But as the computer market matures this argument is becoming less forceful as more and more experienced dealers emerge (often founded by ex-employees of the manufacturers). However not all companies seem to agree with this argument. Digital (DEC), IBM's biggest competitor in the minicomputer market, seem to be going in the opposite direction by enhancing their direct sales operation. And nearly all of the other major players in the minicomputer marketplace (such as ICL, NCR, Olivetti and Unisys) still have direct sales organisations, some even refusing to have dealers at all. And larger manufacturers like IBM and Olivetti also supply microcomputers direct (mainly to major customers who buy in bulk).

It is in very large and complex installations that computer manufacturers come into their own. On these sorts of systems the manufacturers may be your only choice. Even at this level there is yet another example of the tendency towards specialisation – many of the manufacturers have a reputation for being strong in one or two markets, eg NCR, Tandem, IBM and Olivetti in the banking and building society sector, and ICL and NCR in local government systems.

For computer buyers, the question is: given these exceptions, when should I consider a computer manufacturer, and when should I look elsewhere?

THE BENEFITS

You would think that the main advantage of buying from a manufacturer is that as they have built the equipment they should know its capabilities better than anyone. This is generally true, but it has to be remembered that the people you are most likely to be dealing with are sales and marketing personnel. Their knowledge of the equipment's strengths and weaknesses is entirely dependent on the manufacturer's internal training programmes. In addition a substantial proportion of the most popular computers are manufactured outside the UK; therefore any key information has to be transferred to the UK organisation from abroad.

The reason this point is included as a benefit is that most manufacturers manage this flow of information very well. Their sales and marketing staff are generally high-quality people who are able to learn fast and can pass on often highly technical data in a succinct and relevant form. This is especially beneficial in the minicomputer and mainframe market, as this sector is replete with baffling jargon. Indeed, many people are convinced that IBM's marketing motto is 'Keep It Complicated' (based on the theory: 'More complex = more profits').

This hardware knowledge means that once computer manufacturers have discovered what your needs are, they can very quickly tell you which computer in their range best fits these needs. And when it is a vast and complex installation that is being considered, going to a manufacturer may be the only option, as only they have the expertise and knowledge the installation requires. This type of installation, where one organisation handles every aspect of the project (called a 'turnkey' system) is an area where purchase from a manufacturer should be one of the main options considered.

In these large systems the manufacturers obviously have to provide the software as well as the hardware. If the market for a certain type of software is small, or if the production costs are extremely high, it is often only the manufacturers with large research and development budgets and access to worldwide markets that can take on the task in the first place. Only after manufacturers have opened up these areas of the market will smaller companies begin to offer alternatives.

Another major benefit touched on earlier is that manufacturers usually have high-quality, highly-trained staff. As they tend to offer top notch salaries, they naturally attract a substantial proportion of top-quality professional staff. The wide-ranging possibilities for career advancement, and the prestige of working for a major company are also well known incentives for high flyers to join manufacturers. This means that the level of service offered by these companies is usually excellent. However it is worth noting that, similar to computer dealers, as the staff have not been directly involved in the creation of the products, they may occasionally be less committed to their successful implementation than you would expect.

The fact that manufacturers tend to be much more financially reliable than dealers is often uppermost in people's minds when they choose this option. In such a volatile marketplace this is a definite plus point. Even when manufacturers get into difficulty, such as Apple and Apricot did in recent times, they seem more likely to pull through. Both of these companies are now very optimistic about their future prospects, and their account books have a much healthier look.

A final benefit of buying from manufacturers is that if your system breaks down you escape the "it's not our fault, it's the manufacturer" syndrome. Dealers of any sort often make this claim. Sometimes it's true, but mostly it is just a way of ducking responsibility. However, if you are a very small customer of a very large manufacturer, even this may not help. It's not that the manufacturer deliberately ignores your problems. They may genuinely want to help, but their major customers will always get first call on the available resources. On the whole though, manufacturers tend to deal direct only with larger customers, so this problem seldom arises.

In short, these are the main benefits of buying direct from the manufacturer:

- manufacturers are generally experts on their own systems, and can help to short-cut the whole selection process;
- when you require a large and complicated installation, they are usually the best (and sometimes the sole) choice;
- their staff are normally top quality, and give an excellent service;
- manufacturers tend to be more financially reliable than are dealers.

THE DRAWBACKS

The main drawback of buying from manufacturers is that they, not surprisingly, will only offer you their own systems. Their own system may well fit your requirements, but if one of their rivals down the road can offer a similar system that is faster and costs less, they aren't going to tell you about it. This is not to say that a dealer would be any more likely to inform you of their competitors' offerings, but most of the bigger dealers do sell more than one make of computer, giving customers at least a limited choice.

(A further point to note here when making comparisons between dealers and manufacturers: the larger you are, the more likely it is that a manufacturer will offer you a better price; the smaller you are, the more likely it is that a dealer will offer you a better price. This is merely a guideline, *not* a hard and fast rule. And price should only be *one* of many buying criteria.)

Many manufacturers make excellent systems, but very few produce software to match. In fact it is generally only in very specialist areas – such as automated cash machines from IBM and NCR – that manufacturers supply top-quality software. All too often, software offerings are tagged on as an afterthought. Indeed for standard business software for areas such as accounting and word processing, businesses would almost certainly be better going to a dealer for their solution. This means that the benefits of buying from a single manufacturing source are already lost. Some manufacturers don't offer any software at all, apart from the basic operating system. The temptation then is to buy the whole system from the dealer, though not all software houses (companies writing and selling software) sell hardware. Sometimes buying from two or more suppliers is the only solution, and is a fairly common solution in many PC purchases.

A number of manufacturers are not geared up to provide the full support operation required by customers. It also costs substantially less to support experienced dealers than inexperienced customers. And the lack of offices throughout the country is another major drawback. An interesting way to establish whether a manufacturer is serious about supporting their direct sales operation is to check how many offices they have around the country. At least one in London, Birmingham, the Leeds/Manchester area and the Glasgow/Edinburgh area would probably be the bare minimum required.

Another major drawback is the problem of policy changes. If you are an existing customer tied in to one manufacturer, and that manufacturer then drops that particular range of machines, without providing a proper upgrade path to the new range, you can be left in a very tricky position. When Apricot decided to cease production on everything except their new top of the range models, they left behind a lot of irate customers. They tried to make the changeover as painless as possible, and it was motivated by very sound commercial reasoning (and contributed to their financial turnaround), but it still gave a lot of companies a great deal of unwanted hassle.

Similar problems can also arise if you buy from a dealer, but they generally have much more leeway in providing alternatives from other manufacturers. They also have much less financial muscle, and just cannot afford to lose a large batch of customers by leaving them in the lurch. But when someone such as Apricot makes such a radical change in direction, there is little anyone can do to reduce the pain.

A final point, touched on earlier, is that if all you want is one simple, standard PC, you will have a great deal of difficulty in getting it direct from the manufacturer. When it comes to small, low profit systems such as PCs, they are really only interested in selling in volume. Volume usually means a commitment to buy a minimum of 50 PCs in the course of a year. Anything less than this, except in special cases, and they will direct you to a dealer whether you like it or not. Businesses have to be considering minicomputer sized systems before a manufacturer will honour you with their presence for the sale of just one system. Indeed it seems as if some minicomputer manufacturers (such as Digital and NCR) only introduced PC-type systems because their customers forced them to, and that they're not all that interested in selling them (unless they're hooked in to one of their manufacturer systems). So if you want a small quantity of PCs, look for the best dealer in your area.

The drawbacks of buying direct from the manufacturer are:

— they only sell their own machines, limiting your choice;

— they seldom supply quality software to match the computer, so you have to source it from other companies;

— not all manufacturers have true nationwide support operations – vital in many installations;

— a policy change leading to the dropping of a particular range can leave customers high and dry;

— many manufacturers are only interested in supplying systems to major corporate customers.

CONCLUSION

When looked at in greater depth, perhaps in some cases the 'devil you know' is more of a devil than you thought. Clearly, below the level of mainframe systems, it is when a company is considering a large and complex installation that computer manufacturers come into their own. This is not to say that they don't have competition from dealers at this level, but the number of dealers capable of handling such installations is usually limited. With installations being phased in over a period of years, the financial stability factor also increases in importance. But the reason that there are far more dealers than manufacturers is that in most cases (outside the very largest installations) the dealers offer the best combination of skills and expertise.

Most manufacturers realise that this is the reality of the computer market, and design their marketing policies to take account of this. As stated above, a number of them do not even attempt to penetrate this area of the market. However, DEC have had major success in bucking this trend by selling direct. Nothing is simple in the computer maze.

Part 2

Consultancy Companies

5 Accountancy Firms' Consultancy Services

Gamekeepers turned Poachers

GENERAL

Computer consultancy is now one of the major growth areas for accountancy organisations. Under the heading of IT (Information Technology) or management consultancy it is a major source of income for all the big accountancy firms. But it wasn't always like this. The arrival of the PC shook many accountancy firms rigid, especially the smaller organisations. The real blow was the introduction of 'off-the-shelf' accounting software packages. Larger firms had usually been involved in some form of consultancy with their clients so the blow was not as serious for them. But for smaller firms the idea that their clients could now do their own accounts, and not pay them for doing them, was seen as a disaster, and to be avoided at all costs. This led to many short-sighted firms taking rearguard action against the introduction of computerised accounting into their clients' companies. This usually took the form of scare stories along the lines of "You don't know what you're doing and it will just lead to financial disaster for your company".

Of course, in many cases this was in fact true. Most companies can tell stories of the problems they encountered when they first brought computers into their working environment. But it was generally over-emphasised. On the other hand the more far-sighted companies saw a great opportunity opening up, and rapidly moved from gamekeeping to poaching. They looked at it like this: "Computerisation cannot be avoided. But it is going to lead to problems for a number of companies. So instead of resisting it, we should be offering to help them make the right choice – for a fee of course". Many of the major firms who took this attitude have been spectacularly successful. So much so that most of the firms are now complaining of a shortage of qualified staff to handle the ever increasing workloads. And their consultancy operations which started out giving assistance in purely accountancy-based applications now give advice and assistance in almost all areas of computing, including the selection of staff to run the computers ('human resourcing' as personnel work is now called).

But is all this beneficial for the prospective computer buyer, especially considering the large fees charged in most instances?

THE BENEFITS

There may be a degree of argument over what is the major benefit of using an accountancy firm's consultancy service, but many first-time buyers (and second-time buyers who experienced major problems with their first purchase) would probably put 'trustworthiness' high on the list. Some buyers have discovered that certain sections of the maze have degenerated into a savage jungle of rip-off merchants. The services of accountancy firms may not be cheap, but at the very least your chances of getting a working system from a reputable supplier are substantially increased. And if the worst does happen the consultants will help you to recover your costs by building a documented case against the supplier (and not just for your sake: they have their own reputations to consider). The knowledge that you can trust an experienced and (generally) unbiased company to assist you to make the correct decision is undoubtedly a major point to consider when buying a new computer system.

This reputation for independence is obviously of vital importance to the success of these consultancy divisions, but it is clearly not enough on its own to explain the growth of these services. Two other factors which are also important are consultancy services' experience and expertise. This expertise has, in the main, been bought in. The in-house expertise was in general accountancy and audit work. But a combination of good salaries and the prestige of working for big names such as Price Waterhouse, Peat Marwick McLintock, and Arthur Andersen has ensured that these and other firms have been able to attract top-notch staff. (A drawback also has to be considered – most of these employees are CAs who've moved over into IT work; they are *not* all IT professionals such as computer analysts.) The three or four major non-accountancy firms in this field (eg PA Consulting; P-E International; Inbucon) now face competition from all of the big accountancy organisations, which number a dozen or more. But such has been the growth of this market that there is room for them all to prosper. (However, there are rumours that competition is getting so intense that more mergers like the one between Peat Marwick and Thomson McLintock are on the way. Indeed from January 1988 P-E International and Inbucon will be merged in an attempt to match the clout of the leading accountancy-based practices.)

The expertise of these firms has now been largely accepted by the marketplace, and many of the world's leading companies now turn to them for advice and assistance in matters concerning not only immediate computer purchases, but also the formation of future plans for the use of computers and communications. In helping these major firms with their complex problems, most of these consultancy divisions have built up a good amount of experience that can then be related to the needs of their other clients, large and small. Indeed in some cases they are now assisting forward-looking companies to blaze a trail at the forefront of technological innovation, a far cry from their old reputation as boringly safe accountancy audit organisations.

This combination of expertise and experience leads on to the last major benefit of using these services: time saving. By going to these firms for advice, businesses can cut down on the amount of time required to reach a satisfactory conclusion to a computer purchase. They can also gain assistance in working out just what their computer requirements actually are (and whether they require a new system at all). This is especially beneficial when the problems are complex, and would require a substantial amount of internal learning time to be spent before even the requirements could be calculated. Of course, many companies prefer to handle all their problems internally, but there are a steadily growing number who, for whatever reason, look for outside help (not necessarily from accountancy firms) in solving these problems.

To summarise, the main benefits of using accountancy firms'

consultancy services are:

— their 'trustworthiness' – the knowledge that they should be unbiased and should be able to recommend good products and reputable suppliers;

— their expertise – normally due to their quality staff (but often not as high as their public image would suggest);

— their experience – gained from their regular and at times innovative work in the computer world;

— the time saving factor – their knowledge and experience should greatly cut down the time taken to find and install a successful system.

THE DRAWBACKS

From the descriptions above you may be forgiven for thinking that these consultants are as near to perfection in the way they work as you will ever get in the computer maze. But this is not necessarily true, and there are a number of points that business people should be aware of when contemplating spending what can be quite large sums on their consultancy services. The main point to realise is that despite some powerful image-making campaigns in the press (see the *Financial Times* for examples) accountancy firms' consultancy divisions are not all-knowing. And their gleaming public image as unbiased advisors does have a few spots of tarnish (eg a number of firms, such as Arthur Young, are now marketing their own software packages. This step by a few firms into the world of selling is a subject of fierce debate at present).

One of the major failings is laziness. Once an IT consultant has found two or three reputable suppliers, and a couple of good accountancy software packages, the consultant may not look any further, and will just keep giving business to these companies. This may sound OK, but the computer world is very fast moving. Companies and systems change with disturbing rapidity, and if the consultant is not keeping track, then the advice being given to clients may be steadily becoming out-of-date. And if the companies in question know that they are going to get some steady business from the consultant, then their level of service may also begin to decrease, as they know that they don't have to try too hard. In certain isolated cases consultants show far too much favour to certain suppliers, perhaps due to feeling comfortable with them, to the detriment of their clients' interests.

The next drawback that must be considered is the level of IT expertise that a firm has. Not all firms are on the same level, or put as much emphasis on their IT consultancy services. And it has to be remembered that these firms have offices all over the country, and not all these offices reach the same high standards of knowledge. Not too surprisingly, you will sometimes find that a firm that has a tremendous reputation nationally (which means that its London offices are excellent) does not match this image at the local level. This may not be too much of a drawback if this central expertise can be tapped for your benefit, but some of the big firms work on a decentralised basis, with all enquiries handled locally. This means that you are entirely reliant on local expertise, which may or may not be of the same standard.

Smaller local accountancy firms may not have the necessary resources to offer high level computing advice even at their head-quarters. Firms of this type tend to offer advice at the PC level only. Some firms restrict themselves to recommending only one or two market leading packages on market leading hardware in almost all cases. This tends to produce a lot of recommendations for Pegasus accounting software running on IBM PCs – by no means the best choice in every case. This 'safety first' policy hardly justified their often substantial consultancy fees.

This leads on to another important drawback: many inexperienced firms merely pick up some relevant information from certain dealers they know and then just pass it on to their clients. This results in clients paying quite substantial sums for a sophisticated messenger service. The clients would have been better doing some research on their own and then approaching the dealer direct. But the 'safety' factor in using the services of a 'consultant' can have an irresistible pull.

Linked to the points above is a drawback mentioned under 'Benefits': many of the people involved in handing out advice are not IT people, they are CAs who've moved into IT consultancy.

This does not mean that they are incapable of giving very sound advice, but it does indicate that they have a learning curve to traverse. Unfortunately a number of accountancy firms give their trainees consultancy tasks to perform at a very early stage in their development. So while you may think that you are paying for years of experience and expertise, you may be in fact be assisting in the training of a new member of staff. And while this trainee may be fully supervised, this may not be the service you expected. So it pays to enquire about your contact's background, and their number of years in IT consultancy.

The final drawback, and an important one for many companies, is the cost involved. For certain purchases there is a very tight budget set, and these budget strictures may mean that there is only enough money available to buy the system, but not enough to pay for a proper consultancy study to be done. This may appear to be a short-sighted viewpoint, but most managers and buyers will have found themselves in this position at one time or another. There are also a great many people who grudge paying money to outsiders to analyse their business, and in many cases this reluctance is justified. For fairly simple purchases it doesn't really take that much effort to do the business analysis required and to examine the offerings of a number of suppliers. Yet a large number of companies still engage consultants to help them with the purchase of even a single PC.

For more complex and innovative installations it is harder to say when a company should and should not involve a consultancy organisation. The decision must be based on the amount of in-house expertise available, and the timescales involved. For companies with whizz-kid data processing staff, handling the whole project internally can be the best choice. But having good and knowledgeable staff is not the sole consideration, as there is only so much time that they can spend away from their normal work, so the timescale projections have to be closely examined as well.

This does not mean that companies without experienced staff have no option but to turn to some form of consultancy. Again it depends on the staff involved. If your company has people who can pick up new information quickly and effectively, and are good at business needs analysis (which is, after all, a substantial proportion of what computer consultancy work involves) then paying large sums for outside help may be a waste of money. But always remember that you are also paying for computer expertise, and that a depth of computer knowledge cannot suddenly be created out of nothing. One way round this, of course, is to do what the big accountancy firms did: buy in experienced computer personnel and control all your requirements internally.

These are the major drawbacks to using accountancy firms' computer consultancy services:

— the consultant you are dealing with may favour one or two regular suppliers, and may be too lazy (or lack the resources) to go and look for the best supplier for your particular needs;

— the various consultancies have different standards of knowledge, and may lack expertise in certain areas – but they are unlikely to tell you this;

— the local branch that you deal with may not have the same level of expertise as the rest of the firm;

— always remember that you are likely to be dealing with CAs, and not with experienced IT staff;

— the costs involved may not be justified.

CONCLUSION

The spectacular successes mentioned earlier clearly indicate that the accountancy firms' consultancy services are answering definite business needs. Despite the fact that most businesses now have a far higher level of computer knowledge than in the past, more and more companies are turning to consultants for advice and assistance. This is part of a general trend towards specialisation that is affecting many sectors of the computer industry. Many companies now not only bring in outside help to assist them on purchase decisions, but there is also a steadily increasing demand for outside organisations to take over responsibility for the complete project management of the installation once the system has been purchased. (This includes manufacturers such as ICL, as well as consultancy companies.) Indeed, some companies have turned over the entire day-to-day running of their computer installations to outside specialists, such as the Hoskyns Group. The major conclusion to draw from all this is that whether you like it or not consultancy organisations of this type are going to be playing an increasingly important role in the future of Information Technology selection and implementation.

The growth of these organisations should probably be taken as a plus point. Their arrival, plus the general trend towards specialisation throughout the industry, is a pointer towards an underlying development that will be to the benefit of all computer users: the computer market's maturity and stability. The computer manufacturers have been going through some troubled times in the last two or three years, but some market analysts have pointed out that this is not all bad news and that what we are actually witnessing is a market reaching maturity. This results in many of the weaker organisations falling by the wayside. The growth of consultancy services and specialist suppliers is another indicator of this development. Maturity also leads to stability, and it is this stability that allows specialist organisations to grow and prosper.

For computer buyers this is all good news. A market that is stable means continuity of supply, and the growth of expertise. Forward strategies can be developed in the knowledge that supply will continue, and that assistance with planning, selection and installation is available if required. The rapidly expanding accountancy firms' consultancy divisions are at the forefront of this growth in expertise and the demand for their services is undeniable. They most certainly don't have the answers in every case, but many of the largest companies in this country will at least consider using their services when looking for new systems.

The following is a list of some of the larger accountancy firms that offer IT consultancy in the UK:

1 Arthur Andersen

2 Arthur Young

3 Binder Hamlyn

4 Coopers & Lybrand

5 Deloitte Haskins + Sells

6 Ernst & Whinney

7 Grant Thornton

8 Pannell Kerr Forster

9 Peat Marwick McLintock

10 Price Waterhouse

11 Spicer & Oppenheim

12 Touche Ross

6 Management and Business Consultants

Hi-Finance, Low-Tech

GENERAL

There are a great many companies that fall under the description of a management or business consultancy. Only a relatively small proportion of them are able to give useful advice on computer-related subjects. However, a greater proportion than this will in fact claim to be able to give this advice. For prospective purchasers the aim is to seek out the ones which live up to the claims.

Computers are now a central part of business strategy, and this can be confirmed by the development of IT consultancy in most of the accountancy firms' management consultancy divisions. But this does not mean that every company that terms itself a 'management consultancy' knows anything about computers. Indeed it could be said that most of the smaller consultancies are good at business finance and business strategy consultation, but on the whole they are unable to give worthwhile advice on potential computerisation. (There are exceptions to this rule of course.) It is mainly the larger organisations such as PA Consultancy Services, P-E International, Inbucon and BIS that have specialist IT divisions.

So is it useful for prospective buyers to approach these organisations? The answer is probably yes, but you should be aware of their strengths and weaknesses.

THE BENEFITS

The arguments for going to one of the larger organisations for computer consultancy are generally the same as the ones outlined in the previous chapter regarding accountancy firms' consultancy services. But what about the smaller and more local organisations? Are they worth contacting (and paying money to)? The answer is: it depends on your requirements.

These smaller and more local organisations may not on the whole have the greatest expertise on computer systems, and may not be able to give specific advice on which computers to choose, but when you consider that computers are now a standard part of business existence, they can often give some very useful general advice. For smaller companies, and new start-up ventures and first-time buyers in particular, they can offer some important advice regarding the financial costs of a computer system. They should be capable of assisting you to fit a computer system into your general business strategy of profit and growth. This can be very important as the purchase of a new computer system, which can be a very costly item of expenditure, cannot be divorced from standard business decisions. Should you actually buy a new computer?; or expand into new premises?; or invest in new machinery?; or increase your staffing levels?

Management and business consultants should be able to assist you to make these vital business decisions. It may do little to alleviate the problems of unemployment, but companies often find it more cost effective to buy a computer system to aid their expansion than to take on extra staff. It really depends on the market you are in, and the systems that are available.

Being somewhat cut off from the mainstream of computerisation can also be construed as a benefit. If these companies have to do some research into the computing world on your behalf at least they will approach it with (hopefully) an open mind free of prejudice and bias. If they are good at their jobs they should be able to recommend some systems that can do what you require, rather than fall back on old advice that they hand out regularly. This also leads into the question of service.

As with smaller computer dealers, small management consultants can often give a higher level of service than their larger counterparts. Instead of being a small customer of a massive worldwide organisation, you could be one of the larger clients of a local organisation, and may get better treatment because of it. Again similarly to small computer dealers, you can find yourself dealing with senior and experienced executives of an organisation, rather than being palmed off with a trainee as sometimes happens with the larger consultants. In the final analysis it really depends on what you feel comfortable with.

The main benefits of using management and business consultants are as follows:

— good advice about fitting a computer purchase into your general business strategy;

— the larger organisations usually have specialist IT consultancy divisions, with similar benefits to those outlined in the previous chapter;

— their advice should be free of bias;

— you can often receive a higher degree of service from smaller consultancies.

THE DRAWBACKS

The major drawback of management and business consultancies is a lack of knowledge of the computer world. Many of the smaller consultancies can be experts in the financial aspects of business life, with lots of useful advice about locally available grants for machinery and training, but their knowledge of computers can be very limited (almost nil in some cases). This criticism doesn't apply to the larger consultancies such as PA and Inbucon, and most of the smaller organisations will be quite open about their lack of knowledge in these areas, stressing that their strengths lie in other areas of specialisation. However computer consultancy work is a booming business, and some of the less scrupulous outfits may well take on some IT consultancy tasks that they are just not qualified to handle. The best defence against this is to use only those organisations with an established reputation in this field. Asking a prospective consultant what his company's track record is, and for brief career details on the staff who will be handling your assignment, is not a total guarantee of good service, but it can give you much more information on which to base your decision.

Smaller companies, even those with a fair amount of expertise and experience, also face the following related problems: the size of their knowledge base; the cost of information gathering; and holding on to quality staff. The computer consultancy division in a large consultancy can have 50 or more staff members, which allows the creation of specialist subdivisions (such as local government, finance, and manufacturing). This in turn allows the growth of a wide knowledge base that they can work from, with greater in-depth knowledge available for their clients. Even some large management consultancies which have not put a great amount of resources into their computer divisions can be faced with this problem.

With a small staff the best solution is to specialise. But if the management and business sides of the consultancy are geared up to address the problems of the general business world, and this is also where most of the computer work is generated, then the computer staff will also be expected to handle a huge range of potential computer related work, and their knowledge base may not be sufficient to enable them to provide top quality advice and recommendations in all cases. The problem for potential clients is that you are unlikely to be told about this lack of knowledge.

The cost of information gathering, and the sheer time involved, is directly related to this lack of staff. To gather all the information required to be able to offer a proper consultancy service is a mammoth task. And it is a continuous task, as computer technology develops and changes at a tremendous rate. Organisations that approach computer consultancy on a piecemeal basis, without allocating the proper resources to the task, are not able to offer the best advice. How can a consultancy recommend the 'best system' for your business when they may not even be aware that this 'best system' exists? Some of the smaller consultancy outfits may never have owned or used a computer themselves, yet they sometimes attempt to give (costly) advice on the subject.

The larger consultancy organisations with specialist computer consultancy divisions have few problems attracting and holding on to quality staff members. But smaller consultancies, or consultancies who approach computer consultancy work as an afterthought, may not be so lucky. Like any small company, or small division, they can occasionally rely too heavily on one or two key members of staff. If these staff members leave their consultancy service can be hard hit. This again comes back to the question of knowledge base. If the knowledge base isn't spread as widely as possible then the organisation is vulnerable to staff defections, and quality IT staff are in short supply in the UK.

CONCLUSION

The term 'management consultant' can be somewhat misleading, since many accountancy firms' IT consultancy services are part of their management consultancy divisions. The management and business consultants referred to in this chapter are those whose primary (in some cases sole) service is financial and business management advice and assistance; ie non-IT consultants.

Consultancies of this sort are clearly not the best sources of advice on prospective computer purchases. With the exception of some of the larger organisations with specialist IT divisions (who properly belong in the next chapter) they are not really qualified to give IT recommendations. They can often give excellent advice on the financial implications of a computer purchase, but if you really feel you need the assistance of an IT consultant then the type of organisations examined in Chapters 5, 7 and 8 would be of more use to you.

7 Specialist Computer Consultancies

All that Glisters is not Gold

GENERAL

There is a substantial degree of overlap between this chapter and Chapter 3 (Specialist Computer Dealers). This is due to the fact that a large proportion of specialist computer consultants are also dealers for some form of hardware or software. The reason these companies are considered in this chapter and not under Chapter 3 is that they tend to stress their consultancy services over the dealership side of their business. (It should also be remembered that *all* computer consultancies are involved in selling you something, even if it is only their own consultancy services.)

The term 'specialist computer consultant' also requires some clarification. If it is taken to mean an organisation which specialises in independent and unbiased computer consultancy (and related services such as training) across the whole spectrum of the information technology field then there is probably only one company which fits this description: the National Computing Centre. This was set up by the government in 1966 with the aim of promoting the effective use of information technology, and it was originally grant-aided. Today most of its income comes from selling its own products and services in the commercial marketplace, but it is still influenced by 'national interest' considerations alongside the commercial necessities. Part of its remit is to publish books such as this one, which could be considered a sort of indirect consultancy service. The services offered by NCC are wide and varied (and independent!) and anyone interested in availing themselves of these services should contact the NCC direct at its Manchester headquarters, or at any of its regional offices throughout Britain.

This chapter is primarily concerned with organisations that fall under a second definition of the term specialist computer consultant – that is, organisations which offer consultancy services in a niche, or vertical, area of the computer market, such as CAD/CAM (computer-aided design/computer-aided manufacture), the financial markets or POS (point-of-sale) systems. The vast majority of these organisations are commercial companies which also sell hardware or software (often products they themselves have produced).

There are some large organisations who are entitled to the description of specialist, such as CMG (Computer Management Group Ltd), as they have a number of sub-companies which specialise in various areas of the market; for example, retailing, insurance systems, banking and manufacturing industry; Business Intelligence Services Ltd (better known as BIS) who also have a number of specialist sub-companies (insurance; banking); and CACI who have specialist divisions covering system development, analysis and strategy studies; but on the whole specialist computer consultancies tend to be smaller software houses who also offer consultancy services. Examples are Yard in Glasgow (part of the CAP group) who specialise in software for the defence industries; Alkemi (computer security and disaster recovery); and Claremont Controls who are the authors of the Hornet project planning package.

The reason that many of these companies are considered in this chapter is that they have a tendency to include the word 'consultant' somewhere in their name, such as The Quantum Consultancy which offers software for financial markets and bespoke programming; Applied Business Consultants (POS software); and Chess Consultancies (tailored software for transport, warehousing and distribution). The organisations named above are just a brief cross-section of the many companies that offer consultancy services in niche markets.

THE BENEFITS

Specialist computer consultancies should have a sound knowledge of their subject – an above average knowledge; this is what entitles them to the description 'specialist'. If they really are specialist, then they will have built up a base of knowledge in one or two subjects that is wider than most of the other companies competing for your custom. This specialist knowledge should then be available to you in the form of specialist advice – they should know your market, and the computer systems relevant to that market, and be able to advise you on which systems will give the best return to your company. Unfortunately most companies will advise you that their own software or hardware is perfect for your needs. This may or may not be true, but at least they should know your market, and the software they offer should address most of the requirements of companies like yourselves (especially if they have a number of already successful installations).

A few of these consultancies were in fact founded by people who used to work in the commercial environment that they are now trying to advise. The staff in this type of consultancy should know what they are talking about, as long as they have merged computer expertise with their commercial know-how. Most specialist computer consultancies spread their knowledge around a fairly limited market area. Beware of small consultancies who claim to be specialists in many different areas – it is only companies the size of CMG or BIS that can truly make this claim.

In theory, specialist consultancies should be unbiased in their advice and recommendations. In practice it is probably only the NCC itself that reaches this position of commercial purity. As has been stated already, most of these consultancies also supply hardware and software. Even large outfits such as CMG have a distinct tendency to recommend their own products. This is not as much as a drawback as it might at first sight appear. If they are a reputable supplier then they will amend and improve their products over a period of time in line with the demands of their customers. By operating at the sharp end of supply these organisations should have been able to build up a store of good sound commercial experience relating to the needs of their customers. This can often be more beneficial to prospective customers than the exploits of purely consultancy based firms who can often attempt to advise you on hardware or software that they have never set eyes on before. The type of company you choose to do business with finally depends on your own judgement of their skills, but always be aware that the computer maze is coloured in various shades of grey, and that there are very few cases where your choice will be 'black or white'.

These, then, are the major benefits of using the services of specialist computer consultants:

- they should have a sound knowledge of your market sectors' computerisation needs;
- they are able to offer specialist advice;
- the best organisation will have reacted to customer suggestions and improved their products;
- they should have allied good commercial experience to their existing knowledge.

THE DRAWBACKS

The idea of going to a specialist consultancy organisation may, on first consideration, appear to be the best route through the maze for companies facing the problematic decision of which computer system to choose. But as the paragraphs above suggest, there are very few companies which actually live up to the description specialist computer 'consultant' if you take that term to mean 'unbiased advisor'. This is a misused, and often deliberately misleading claim, as most 'specialist consultancies' are in reality no more than ordinary specialist *sales* organisations. If an unbiased advisor is what you are in fact looking for, then the companies discussed in Chapters 5 and 8 (for IT advice) and Chapter 6 (for general IT/financial advice) are probably better bets. Once this fact has been recognised it becomes clear that the drawbacks to using the services of this type of organisation are very similar to those outlined in Chapter 3 (Specialist Computer Dealers). For an in-depth look at these drawbacks refer to Chapter 3 – there is little that can be added here that would not cover exactly the same ground.

The following is a slightly modified version of the summary of the drawbacks that appears in Chapter 3:

- a number of consultants use the term 'specialist' purely as a marketing ploy – they may have no more specialist knowledge than other consultancies;
- 'specialist' knowledge can also mean 'limited' knowledge of other market areas – beware of stepping outside your advisor's area of specialisation;

— specialist consultants, if they are really disguised dealers, can be prone to the winds of market change (if they are true consultants then they should not only avoid this, but should also be able to help you avoid buying out-of-date equipment);

— as specialist consultants are usually also selling their own products, they will tend to be more biased than other 'true' consultancy organisations.

CONCLUSION

As was stated in the Introduction to this book, the fact that most specialist computer consultants are actually rather poorly disguised sales organisations is not necessarily a bad thing. As long as you are aware of this potential bias, then these organisations can indeed be very useful to you in your search for computer solutions. True specialist knowledge is often at a premium in the computer world, and the fact that many of these organisations are in possession of this knowledge can outweight their other obvious drawbacks. The task for the potential buyer is to sift out the useful bits of specialist knowledge from the chaff of self-promotion bias.

8 Public Funded Consultancies

No Axe to Grind?

GENERAL

There are very few computer consultancies that are completely public funded. 'Public subsidised' would perhaps be a better and more accurate description as many of the consultancies analysed in this chapter are, in reality, limited company offshoots of educational establishments. This situation has arisen as university and college budgets have been squeezed, and these establishments have sought new ways to raise cash. Jumping on the computer consultancy bandwagon has been one popular method. These academic-based consultancies, however, are normally staffed by employees of the education establishments, and tend towards a far greater degree of specialisation than your average commercial consultancy.

Here are a few examples of these 'public subsidised' organisations:

Aberdeen University Engineering Services Ltd (specialise in electrical, mechanical and civil engineering)

Bradford University Software Services Ltd (scientific and engineering research; graphics)

Computing Services (University of Glasgow) Ltd (scientific research)

Humberside College of Higher Education (engineering; production control)

Abacus, Department of Architecture, University of Strathclyde (computer-aided architectural design, construction and building)

Salford University Business Services Ltd (manufacturing and electronics)

University of Kent Computing Laboratory (education)

There are also subsidiary consultancy operations operated by other government bodies, such as Clydeport Data Management Ltd – an offshoot from the Clydeport Authority – which offers consultancy services in the field of public administration.

Some examples of true public funded consultancies are:

The National Engineering Laboratory (funded by the Department of Industry, and specialising in structural analysis and numerically controlled machine tools)

The Scottish and Welsh Development Agencies (which have specialist computer consultancy divisions)

Local Better Business Schemes (which allow companies to approach private sector consultancy companies with partial payment for their services through a grant scheme)

The details above are a brief overview of the organisations that operate in this sector. The rest of this chapter looks at the strengths and weaknesses of these organisations.

THE BENEFITS

The main benefit of these organisations is that they tend to offer consultancy services in areas that are inadequately covered by most commercial consultancies. This is especially true of the offshoots of educational establishments which are strong in areas like computer-aided design and manufacture, and the scientific and engineering disciplines. Organisations such as the SDA and WDA also have divisions which were created to assist new companies in choosing and integrating computers into their company structure.

To a large extent these organisations should be unbiased in their recommendations, and do qualify for the 'no axe to grind' label, but be wary of tie-ups and 'sponsorship agreements' with certain computer manufacturers, as these consultancies may have a tendency to recommend their sponsors' products. The consultancy services offered by the SDA and WDA are very useful for new ventures, and they have a good reputation for successful recommendations, but unfortunately there is no equivalent organisation in England (a source of political discontent in certain 'deprived' English regions).

For companies who are looking for research work at the forefront of technology, then consideration of the services offered by these establishments should be high on your list of prospects. Indeed many of the so-called consultancy services that academic and government bodies claim to supply is really only of secondary importance to these organisations, whose primary interest is research. For organisations that lack the time or the money to carry out their own research projects, the services offered by public funded consultancies can be very cost effective.

To summarise, these are the main benefits of public funded consultancies:

- their strengths often lie in areas which are inadequately covered by commercial consultancy organisations;
- grant-aided schemes are very cost effective for new companies;
- they are generally unbiased in their assessments and recommendations;
- they are one of the best sources for research-based consultancy work.

THE DRAWBACKS

Unfortunately 'public funded' is often a euphemism for 'short funded'. Many of these organisations could offer a far superior service if they had more funds available to them. In some cases it is only this lack of funds which have driven academically-minded researchers to offer consultancy services to the commercial world, and some still view it as a regrettably necessary intrusion on their real research work. This leads to a lower level of service for their customers than they would expect to receive.

This lack of funds also means that the payment levels for staff are lower than those available in commercial companies. While this may irritate many of the most dedicated employees of these organisations, it does not mean that they are going to leave. Unfortunately this is not true in all cases and there tends to be a steady drain of good quality staff to the commercial world. This again can affect the level of consultancy work on offer.

A complaint often laid against these organisations is that as most of their staff have spent practically all of their working lives in an academic or governmental workplace, how can they possibly be in a position to give advice to commercial companies? There is a certain amount of truth in this claim, but all of these organisations are being forced to improve their commercial awareness, whether they like it or not, so this is a problem whose impact is steadily decreasing. However, it can be worthwhile enquiring about the backgrounds of the staff in these organisations, just to see how many of them have had commercial experience. The staff in these organisations can often be at the sharp end of research, but they are seldom at the sharp end of commercial applications.

These are the drawbacks associated with public funded consultancies:

— they can often be short of the funds necessary to do their work properly;

— they may be lacking commercially aware staff;

— their knowledge base may be too heavily research-based for it to be useful to many commercial organisations.

CONCLUSION

Public funded consultancies should certainly be considered for general consultancy work (for one thing they will probably be cheaper than most of the large commercial organisations), but it is really in the areas of specialist consultancy and research-based consultancy that they come into their own. As the list of consultants at the start of this chapter suggests, their strengths lie in the scientific, engineering and design fields – areas which are often neglected by the commercial organisations. The fact that they also tend to be less biased than many other 'specialist' consultancies is an added bonus.

In short, companies with an interest in utilising consultancy services in these disciplines should give public funded consultancies serious consideration.

Part 3

Information Sources

9 The Computer Press

Widgets and Gizmos, Bells and Whistles

GENERAL

As befits a burgeoning market, there is no shortage of computer magazines and newspapers which attempt to give prospective buyers advice. Unfortunately there is a shortage of publications which get to grips with real business needs. Many of the more heavyweight journals are aimed at the computer trade itself, or at experienced users in DP (data processing) departments in large companies, and not at hard-pressed business buyers. And most of the journals supposedly attempting to assist business people are more concerned with delving into the innards of the machines. In some magazines it is all widgets and gizmos, bells and whistles, with scant concern shown for their proper business applications. So what if one machine is *x* Mhz faster than another, and has two extra bits and bobs? The real question is: can it do the job?

Therein lies the problem. Most business needs are very specific. However, in order to sell in large volumes, most journals are generalist in tone and content. This means that as information sources computer journals have to be used carefully and selectively. They are only a part of the complex whole that is the computer maze. For people new to the market, or new to a particular sector of the market, journals are best at giving a general overview of what is available. They can help to point prospective buyers in the correct direction. But be wary of specific recommendations in magazines; they are often wrong, or have reached a conclusion based on factors important to the writer, but which may not be important to you. Remember that these reviews are written by journalists who have deadlines to meet (and seem sometimes to lack commercial experience).

This is not to say that these publications do not perform a very useful role. They do churn out masses of information on a regular basis, information that may be unavailable elsewhere. The trick is to select the bits that are relevant to you. Often they come into their own *after* you have bought a system, by keeping you up-to-date with any new developments that may affect you or your system, such as the recent major changes in direction by Apricot and IBM at the PC level. But there are an awful lot of publications in existence. Which one(s) should an interested buyer choose? This is not an easy question to answer, as there is a great deal of overlap between the competing journals, but the specific piece of information you need may be outside this overlap.

The aim of this chapter is to give general guidance on the various types of journals available, and to assist you in the process of selecting which publications may be of use. For ease of understanding, the computer press can be categorised under four headings, the main one being the target market. The others are the type of publication; the type(s) of machines covered; and the software applications covered. All of these criteria relate back to the targeted readership.

1 *Target Market*

- a The inexperienced public
- b Experience users and people in the computer trade
- c Specialists
- d Academics

2 *Type of Publication*

- a Newspapers
- b Magazines
- c Special business publications
- d Academic publications

3 *Machines Covered*

- a Personal computers
- b Minicomputers
- c Mainframe computers (DP departments)
- d Specialist computers

4 *Software Applications Covered*

- a General business applications
- b Specific business applications
- c Academic and research applications

The aim of this chapter is not to give an exhaustive listing of all the computer journals available (there are other books, such as the *Computer Users' Year Book*, that attempt this) but to discuss some of the major publications on the market. The categorisation outlined above is helpful as a framework on which to build an understanding of the range and usefulness of the multitude of publications available.

JOURNALS FOR THE INEXPERIENCED USER

Most of the journals for the inexperienced user are published in magazine format, and they tend to be the most generalist of all. They are mostly monthly publications, but *PC Week* claims to be the only weekly newspaper in this sector of the market. Some of the leading publications for inexperienced users are (see also Appendix 1, Bibliography):

Micro Decision

PC User

PC Week

Personal Computer World

Practical Computing

What Micro?

Which Computer?

The publishers of these journals are faced with something of a dilemma – most of their readers don't really know what they want, so they have to print generalist articles to satisfy all needs. But at the same time, a substantial proportion of their readers have very specific needs that they also have to satisfy. They attempt to answer this dichotomy by publishing general news items alongside in-depth surveys of particular sectors of the market. But on the whole it is the buckshot approach to business requirements: write enough articles on a huge spread of issues and you're bound to cover something of interest to nearly everyone. Because of this it is possibly best, if you have the time, to keep an eye on the publications as they come into the newsagents and to have a quick scan through them to see if they have any in-depth studies that are relevant to your needs. (You will often find groups of people standing in newsagents doing just that!)

Despite these criticisms, it should be recognised that these magazines are very professionally produced and do contain some nuggets of information that are important to prospective computer buyers. But these nuggets have to be dug out. For example, these magazines continually produce articles reviewing the latest models from the computer manufacturers. But this process has both strengths and weaknesses. The plus point is that these articles may well tell you things that the sales organisations never would, like the fact that many of the manufacturers' new products are not fully compatible with their existing products, or even with the existing standards. The great drawback, however, is that these new products have never been tested in the real world, so any conclusions they come to have to wait on the final judgement of computer buyers to see if the reviews were right (or wrong, as the case may be).

A perfect example was the launch of the original IBM PC. A substantial number of these magazines fulminated against its very existence, saying that it was a machine built with technology that was already out-of-date, and that many of the other machines available at that time were far superior in design. Perhaps this was true, but it didn't stop the IBM PC from rapidly becoming the dominant machine in the PC marketplace. The reality was that business buyers were buying IBMs because of the reliability factor, and not because it was faster or slower than other machines.

These magazines are useful for new buyers who want to gain an understanding of the computer world at PC level. (This is an important point. After reading most of these magazines you might be surprised to learn that businesses use anything other than PCs.) But their main use is for businesses that already own PCs. When it comes to keeping existing users up-to-date with new developments in the PC world they are unrivalled. The best bet is to choose one of the magazines which is written in a style that you like and to stick with it. A quick scan down the contents page for any articles that may be of particular interest, plus a look over the news pages is usually sufficient to keep you abreast of any new developments that may affect your business. This is, in fact, just what many of the people in the PC computer trade do every month.

JOURNALS FOR THE EXPERIENCED USER

For some reason known only to the marketing companies, most of these publications are in newspaper format, unlike the journals for the inexperienced user. The exception is the heavyweight (in both senses) computer journal *Byte*. This is produced in the USA, but has a respectable circulation in the UK. It is a very technically-minded publication aimed at what is termed a 'computer-literate' readership. Its published conclusions are usually authoritative and accurate, but due to its relatively low circulation these views are not widely disseminated. It is worth picking up a copy from a newsagent just to see if you like the style. Most of the other publications mentioned are free to readers who meet certain qualifying criteria, but you probably won't find them in the shops; they are almost all subscription only publications.

Some of the leading newspapers for experienced users are:

Computing

Minicomputer News

Computer Talk

Computer Weekly

The first two are the most news orientated of the publications. *Computing* has by far the largest circulation of the two, and is designed to be a vehicle for news and analysis, mainly for the data processing (DP) world. This means that most of its articles are aimed at mini and mainframe users and not at PC users. *Minicomputer News*, in contrast, has a section at the back of the newspaper specifically covering PC-type systems.

Computer Talk is aimed at DP professionals, and attempts to analyse the needs of computer users, and to suggest solutions to these needs. *Computer Weekly*, with a far higher circulation, caters for both users and suppliers, and includes information on microcomputers. However, the fact that over 50% of the publication is given over to computer job adverts will give some idea of which market sector the publishers hope to reach.

One of the most useful publications is *PC Dealer*, but it may also be one of the hardest to lay your hands on. As its title suggests it is aimed at personnel in PC dealerships, and attempts to cover all of the new developments in the dealership world. A large proportion of the news it carries would also be of interest to anyone considering the purchase of a new system, but the journal has a 'controlled' circulation: ie it is only supposed to be distributed free to senior personnel in dealerships, but you can get it sent to you if you are willing to pay the annual subscription.

As the title of this section suggests, none of the above publications cater for inexperienced users or first-time buyers. They all assume that their readers are already computer users, and they often slip into jargon and into complex terminology. So they are not much use for people who are just out for the computer journal reader's equivalent of a Sunday stroll, but if you want to keep up-to-date with the complexities of the highways and byways of the computer maze then a subscription to at least one of them (as stated above, often free to business users) is probably necessary.

SPECIALIST JOURNALS

There are a great many journals that could be included under this heading, so the aim of this section is just to give a brief overview of some of the publications that may be of interest. These journals can be grouped under four subheadings:

1 Journals aimed at users of specific computers, such as *Apricot User; DEC User*; and *IBM Computing Today*

2 Journals aimed at users of specific software systems, such as *CAD/CAM International*

3 Publications concentrating on a particular sector of the market, such as *Communications Magazine*

4 Journals which are compendiums of information, such as the NCC's *Computing Decisions*

Many of the major makes of computer have journals which concentrate on the users of their machines. This type of publication is most prevalent at the home computer end of the market, but there are a fair number around aimed at business users, ranging from PC systems up to minis and mainframes. The great advantage of these magazines is that they can examine specific issues in much greater depth than the generalist publications. However there are two big drawbacks to this type of publication: firstly, they depend on the manufacturers' machines for their very existence, so if they write too many bad news stories they may be cutting their own throats, and this can lead to a reduction in impartial reporting; secondly, they can spend too much time discussing the merits of one manufacturer and not enough time analysing what may be major changes in the rest of the computer world. The best of these magazines try to avoid these faults, but it is not all that easy to do. Perhaps the best solution is to buy one of these magazines plus a copy of a good generalist publication to get the best of both worlds.

These problems are less likely to arise for journals which are aimed at specific software packages, because they can analyse the benefits and drawbacks of packages that run across a whole range of machines. For anyone wanting a greater insight into the potential of existing packages, and to keep up-to-date with new developments, these magazines can be very useful. They can often suggest ways of improving your return from packages that you are already using. However they do tend towards highly technical discussions, and are only really worth the money if you or someone in your organisation is keen enough to spend the time to read them and to implement any suggestions they may come up with. Too many people buy these publications because they feel they ought to, and they end up lying in reception to be read only by visiting sales representatives.

The journals aimed at very specific sectors of the market are usually highly technical publications written for people with an academic turn of mind. They are of little use to inexperienced users, but for people who are serious about increasing their level of computer knowledge they should be considered. But because of their highly specialist nature they tend to have the lowest circulation of all the journals on the market. This is probably inevitable, but is a bit of a pity as they often have articles written by some of the leading experts in their fields, the people who are designing the systems that many of us will be using in the future.

The NCC publication *Computing Decisions* is a very good example of what is meant by compendiums. Its aim is to be an all-in-one guide to computing, and to assist business people in making computing decisions. It contains sections covering topics such as a list of computer suppliers, editorial contributions offering guidance on decision criteria and salary surveys. There are a number of these directories available, a substantial proportion of them published by the NCC (the *Microsystems Training Directory*, and the *Guide to Computer Aided Engineering Manufacturing and Construction Software*, being two further examples). They can be very useful when considering the purchase of a new system, but are not really designed to be used in isolation, as they do not replace the journals which provide up-to-date news of the rapidly changing computer world. They can, however, save a great deal of time that could otherwise be spent searching for a supplier organisation.

ACADEMIC JOURNALS

There is no shortage of publications of this type, but they tend to be of little use to business buyers as they normally concentrate on new developments that are not yet commercially available, and they are usually written in a very dry style. But for anyone taking a serious interest in computing they could be considered. Try contacting your nearest university's or college's computer department and see if they can help you.

CONCLUSION

With the growth of computer technology, the dissemination of news and information is no longer solely the preserve of the computer press. A number of national newspapers, such as *The Guardian* and *The Times*, now have technology sections (though *The Guardian's* 4-page section on Thursdays leans too heavily towards home computing), and they make far greater attempts to cover the latest developments in computing. The best coverage is probably in the *Financial Times*, which regularly prints extra sections with in-depth analysis of varying topics, including new technology, perhaps the most useful of all being its surveys of computer usage in businesses in the UK and abroad. It's always interesting to know if you are keeping up with the Jones's of the business world.

In addition, many other magazines, such as *Office Equipment News*, and various business trade publications carry articles on different aspects of new technology and computing. So these days there is no shortage of information available if you care to look for it. With so much analysis freely available it makes sense to utilise it when considering a computer purchase. The main decision to make is which journals to buy. This probably depends on three main criteria:

The type of system you are proposing to purchase

Your present level of knowledge

The time available for study

There will probably be two or three journals which will be useful for you, but if this seems like too much, at the very least a perusal of one of the generalist publications will give you an insight into what's happening in the computer maze. Many business people consider that the information they supply about what your market sector rivals are buying is one of computer journals' most useful functions. (See the section on 'Journals for the Experienced User' – these publications, with 'recent orders placed' columns, are often the best source of this type of commercial information.)

10 Books and Manuals

A Little Knowledge Can Be Useful

GENERAL

Books and manuals are probably the simplest, least expensive, and least time-consuming way of increasing your knowledge of the world of computers. They have the added advantage that they can be studied away from the hustle and bustle of a normal office environment, and they also form a permanent store of information that can be returned to when necessary.

Too many people try to improve their knowledge level of computing without ever opening a single book. They appear to think that it would be too laborious to wade their way through a morass of complex information. This attitude ignores the simple fact that there are a great many publications produced with the busy business executive in mind – simple to read; easy to understand; and full of concise and useful information. This style of publication would normally fall under the heading of 'Directories and Guides' which forms the first part of this chapter.

Part two analyses the usefulness of training manuals and 'How To . . .' books. This type of publication has been very successful in the home computer market, with the production of books which explain how to get the best out of various home computers such as the Sinclair series, the BBC Micro and the various Amstrad machines. This format is now regularly used in books which aim to guide first-time users through business micro software packages, especially word-processing systems.

The more formal style of computer books which aim to impart a greater amount of in-depth and usually more complex information is analysed in part three. This type of publication (such as this book itself) usually demands more of the reader, but consequently should also be more rewarding, and should supply the reader with far more useful information (especially on complex subjects like office automation and programming).

A final point to consider: books and manuals are almost certainly the most independent and unbiased sources of information available to computer buyers, quite a rare thing in the computer maze. Reference should also be made to Appendix 1 (*Bibliography*).

DIRECTORIES AND GUIDES

These are extremely useful publications which range from simple lists of information about PC systems and suppliers up to more sophisticated and detailed guides to various sectors of the computer market. They are used by computer suppliers as well as users as handy reference guides to what is available in the computer world. Most large companies with computer sections will have at least one of these publications in their reference book collection. The following list is a very brief cross-section of some of the directories that are available:

The PC Year Book (VNU Business Publications)

The Computer Users' Year Book (VNU)

The Software User's Year Book (VNU)

The Software Guide for Accountants (VNU)

Communications Users Yearbook (Manor House Press)

The Data Comms Book (VNU)

Guide to Computer Aided Engineering, Manufacturing and Construction Software (NCC)

Oxford Survey in Information Technology (Oxford University Press)

Wharton's Complete Guide to Office Automation (Wharton Information Systems)

As you can see from this list, VNU Business Publications have made a speciality of producing very useful and readable directories, especially *The Computer Users' Year Book,* a 3-volume guide to the world of computing. These directories are not cheap (normally they cost £30 plus) but they are packed with useful information. An important point to remember, however, is that these directories are never entirely accurate. In particular under the heading of 'Suppliers' they will have included most of the national names, but they are usually fairly weak at listing all of the local dealers in the country (and the local dealer may be just the one you're looking for). They may not give the exact solution you require, but they should be able to point you in the correct direction.

This 'short-cutting' of the selection process is the most useful application of these directories. For a start they can tell you if there are any companies that can supply the sort of hardware and software that you are looking for. They provide a list of company names and addresses, and often a short summary of the main strengths of a supplier's product. They can also give you new ideas by their coverage of topics that perhaps you hadn't considered before. But these publications are not only bought by prospective buyers – many companies buy them year after year as they are a very good way of keeping up-to-date with the ever-changing layout of the computer maze.

Their directory format also addresses one of the main complaints of busy business executives: the difficulty they sometimes have in finding the information they require in a large complex book. The directories and guides are explicitly laid out in sections, usually with alphabetical listings of entries, so that the information they contain can be accessed quickly and efficiently. The more specialised publications such as *The Data Comms Book* and *Wharton's Complete Guide to Office Automation* usually have more complete listings, as well as greater detail of suppliers' products, and can be very useful for buyers with specific requirements.

In short, directories and guides of this type are a very useful addition to a company's bookshelf.

MANUALS

These books range from the simpler 'How To . . .' style, such as

Getting Started With WordStar from the Oxford University Press and *Using The Amstrad Word Processor* from the NCC, up to the more complex proper training manuals such as the prestigious *SSADM Manual* from the NCC and *The Unix System User's Handbook* from Prentice-Hall International. This type of book is not really of much use to prospective buyers (especially the heavier academic textbook style of publication) but it is useful to be aware that such books exist. The fact that outside help is available makes some first-time buyers feel more confident at stepping into the computer maze.

BOOKS

Computer books can be usefully subdivided into two categories: books for business computer buyers and users; and specialist books (academic; educational; research). Specialist books are only for those people who wish to expand their knowledge beyond that normally required of business executives. Most people probably wouldn't even consider buying a book before buying a computer, but you may be surprised at the variety of useful publications that are available today. For example, the following list is a cross section of some of the titles available from just one publisher (in this case the NCC* – which is probably the main publisher of this type of book in the UK):

Desktop Publishing with the Amstrad PCW

Computerisation Guidelines

Management Guide to Choosing and Implementing Computer Systems

Using Computers – A Manager's Guide

Automating Your Office

Practical Programming for Non-Computer Professionals

Management Guide to Office Automation

This type of book can be extremely useful for business executives

* A book catalogue is available from NCC on request.

who are trying to grasp the concepts and consequences involved in planning and implementing computer projects within their organisations. The list of publications of this sort is growing daily, and there is a steadily increasing number of books which give in-depth analysis on particular subjects which are of interest to business users. Two examples are: *Infotrends – profiting from your information resources*, and *The Information Weapon – winning the customers and markets with technology*, both available from John Wiley and Sons.

There is now a growing belief that while in the past it was having full control of your capital that was the key to growth, in the late-1980s and early-1990s the new key to growth is the efficient use of information. Computers allow you to increase control and effective use of your company's information base, and computer books also have a vital part to play in increasing the level of your knowledge and that of your company. Managers with a clear understanding of current and possible future trends in the information technology sector will have a major role in keeping their companies in profit and ahead of the competition. Regular purchase of computer magazines and books has a central part to play in building and sustaining your level of IT knowledge.

CONCLUSION

The major benefits of books and manuals are:

- directories are short-cuts to computer solutions;
- the information contained in books is generally independent and unbiased;
- specialist information can be gained, and held for future reference;
- books offer a very inexpensive route to self-training, which is non-disruptive as it can be done out of office hours;
- knowledge of Information Technology is vital to every company's future.

There are also some drawbacks which have to be considered:

- some books *can* be very laborious to read;

- there are not enough proper buyer's guides (though this situation is slowly improving);
- buying too many books and magazines can lead to the reader being swamped by a mass of complex (and often contradictory) information;
- some books which attempt to deal with subjects which are at the forefront of technology can become out-of-date very quickly.

On the whole the benefits far outweigh the drawbacks, and adding a few books to the other texts a company possesses is strongly recommended.

11 Seminars and Courses

Back to School

GENERAL

It has been said that British businesses put too little emphasis on training compared to our counterparts abroad, but you would hardly believe it when you see the number of organisations that now offer IT training, and consider the large quantity of courses available from these organisations. Of course it could be argued that the problem lies not so much in computer training, (IT being an 'in' subject and therefore getting a lot of publicity) but in other areas of 're-training' for new technology. Whatever the reason, you will not be stuck for choice when it comes to selecting a training organisation.

IT training ranges from simplistic introductions to PCs, up to computer management courses for senior personnel. For prospective trainees the decision of which course to try depends on your present level of knowledge, and the level you wish to attain, and this chapter gives an overview of the various courses available.

Another information source similar to the training course, but generally much less intensive, is the seminar. There always have been business seminars of one sort or another, and at the end of this chapter there is a survey of the sort of seminars that may be useful to computer buyers, along with a brief look at the usefulness of computer exhibitions as an information source.

TRAINING COURSES

Computer training courses generally fit under one of the following five headings:

Courses giving an Introduction to Computers

Higher level PC Hardware training and Software Package Usage training

Programming and Operating Systems training

Specialist training (Engineering; Scientific; Technical)

Training in the Management of Computer Systems and Projects

The 'Introduction to Computers' training courses are obviously aimed at first-time users. For a business that has a very clear idea of what system they want this type of course is of limited use. It would be far better to get in-depth training on your new system as it was installed. But for people who don't really know what they want, and find the whole world of computing to be confusing, courses such as this can be very helpful. They are usually what is known, in another piece of jargon, as 'hands-on' courses. This means that you get to use a computer as you learn, but beware of courses that are run by companies using home computers like the BBC micro: make sure they train you on a system that is used by businesses (such as IBM, Compaq, Olivetti, Apricot and other IBM-compatible machines).

Although there are some courses giving training up to DP level, most of the introductory style of training is PC based (the assumption being that when you move onto larger systems you already have had some computing training or experience), and the choice of training establishment is wide and varied. The following list is merely a small cross-section of the diverse types of organisations that offer introductory training:

The Instruction Set

Consultancy Firms (eg Arthur Young)

BIS Applied Systems

Computer Training and Education Centre

The Institute of Chartered Accountants

Computer Manufacturers (eg IBM, Olivetti)

Computer Dealers (eg MBS, Computacenter)

Colleges

Government Sponsored ITeC's

The National Computing Centre

Practically all of the organisations named above also offer courses which train users on how to get the best use out of PCs and software packages. Obviously you should not look for training on software packages until you have bought one, or are sure you are going to buy a particular one. In addition most of these organisations' training courses are standard and are set many months in advance, so you should check on the availability of courses before proceeding. Often the best solution is to organise a special course from the organisation that supplied the software to your company. Indeed the main use of such courses is for people who decide that they are not getting the best out of a package they already own, or for companies who wish to train other members of staff on an existing system.

It is interesting to note that the organisations you would expect to be at the forefront of this type of training, namely the universities and colleges with their large teaching staffs and their existing base of IT knowledge, generally arrived rather late on the IT training scene. Indeed in many cases this late arrival wasn't even due to belated enterprise, but was caused by money pressures and the desperate search for new sources of revenue. For this reason it sometimes pays to be wary of the courses offered by your local education establishments – some of the courses on offer betray this haphazard process of creation, and often display a disturbing lack of commercial awareness. This assessment only applies to a small proportion of the courses on offer, but an initial check on the background to the creation of the course would not go amiss.

In addition to the groups named previously, the software houses that wrote the packages also give training on their use. Their courses have benefits and drawbacks. As they wrote the software they obviously should know it very well, but if they were not involved in the sales process that led to the system being installed then they may not know what elements of their software are important to you. The courses available from this type of organisation are often very generalist in tone and content, as they try to be all things to all users, it is quite common to hear attendees complain that the areas they were most interested in were inadequately covered. And if you want a training course which has been specifically designed for your company, then it may prove quite costly to get the software house to do this. In any case you should check that the company you wish to supply your system is capable of giving in-depth training on all aspects of the system, if at all possible (in some of the more complex installations involving more than one supplier this will not be the case).

Computer buyers are not normally interested in programming, but for anyone who wants to develop in-house programming skills there is quite a wide choice of courses available. There are of course the full-time courses at universities and colleges, but there are also a number of organisations which provide anything from introductions to programming, to fully comprehensive programming skills development courses, over a much shorter timescale than the academic institutions. Companies such as ADM, the Hoskyns Group and Olivetti (among numerous others) run these shorter courses which may fit in better with commercial timescales. It is fairly common for staff with general computing qualifications to be sent on a course which gives them in-depth training on a specific programming language which their employer's computers use.

For companies that do not have in-house programming skills, the key question is: does this lack of skill hold back our computer systems' development? Having this type of staff can be expensive, and it is generally only the companies with large mini and mainframe installations that take on programming staff. But there is a lot to be said for companies that are not well served by existing software offerings taking on staff to develop new programs, even in the PC world. This is not a simple decision to make, as businesses must balance the costs involved with the potential benefits.

Companies with specialist computer systems, such as those used for Engineering; Scientific Work; Graphics; CAD (Computer-Aided Design); and Technical Analysis will probably have to either take on specialist staff to operate and develop the systems, or to train existing members of staff to use the systems. Organisations such as Will-Denn Resources, BIS Applied Systems, Systems Designers and the Cranfield Institute of Technology offer courses to train or re-train staff in these disciplines. Any company which is considering the purchase of a specialist system would also investigate the internal resources available for the operation of the system and to allow for training costs if there is a lack of skills.

The training courses in the 'Management of Computer Systems' are generally aimed at larger systems in the mini and mainframe markets and cover topics such as how to control the growth of computerisation, DP management development, system administration and project planning and management. Organisations such as BIS Applied Systems, manufacturers such as Digital, and the NCC offer training courses of this type. Any companies that are experiencing rapid growth will probably have a need for training of this type. It is of course essential that managers' levels of skill are kept up to scratch as well as the staff they manage. There is a tendency in some companies to offer excellent introductory training to new members of staff, but to neglect the future development of the skills of their managers. When it comes to the running of computer systems, which are usually a significant investment and can often be the financial heart of your business, this could be a very costly omission.

CONCLUSION

One of the main criticisms levelled at British businesses is that they do not offer enough re-training to existing members of staff. Considering the often large financial investment companies make in gaining and retaining staff this is a short-sighted attitude. In the continually changing world of electronics and computers it could be very damaging to a company's prospects of survival to let your employees' skill levels fall too far behind that of your competitors. So training as an information source is potentially useful for first-time buyers, but it is an area that every company that uses computers has to examine very closely to make sure that you are keeping up with technology. Computers do not solve problems on their own, they are merely tools to be used by businesses, and keeping managers and staff well trained makes the purchase of a new system easier as there should be a wealth of in-house expertise to draw on when analysing the requirements and the potential new systems on offer.

Most of the training companies should also be able to offer advice on the range of training grants available. Anyone having difficulty finding information on this subject should contact the NCC.

SEMINARS

The vast majority of the seminars that are open to the public are thinly disguised sales pitches, but they should not be dismissed out of hand because of this. As long as attendees are aware of this a great deal of useful information can be picked up at these meetings. The non-sales type are usually run by institutes such as the British Computer Society, or by independent bodies like the NCC, and are members-only affairs (often distinguished by being called conferences).

Most computer dealers have run seminars at one time or another, on a variety of subjects, and if you are considering the purchase of a system you should consider attending one or two, as long as the subject matter is relevant. At the very least you should gain some more information than you already had, and as a bonus you can gain an understanding of the size and business philosophy of potential suppliers. In most cases (but *not* always) a professionally presented seminar probably means that there is a professionally run company behind it. These seminars are run under a great variety of titles such as: a CAD Seminar or named after some other application package; a dealer's Open Day; a Visitors' Day – such as IBM run at their Greenock manufacturing plant; or a New Product Launch, which often take place at a prestigious location such as a well-known hotel.

There has also been a massive increase in the number of seminars run during general computer exhibitions. During a 3-day exhibition visitors could attend anything up to 15 seminars if they were really keen. In reality only one or two will be relevant, and it may be worthwhile to attend them, as seminars of this type are often planned months in advance and can contain some very useful information.

The organisers of members-only seminars run by institutes and societies usually have the benefit of knowing what sort of information is relevant to their members and can therefore make sure that the content will be of interest. In addition they can invite along some outside experts as well as some reputable suppliers. Often some members will be willing to explain what their experiences have been in purchasing and installing new systems.

Obviously there is a limit to the number of seminars that business people can attend, but if you wish to increase your level of knowledge before purchasing a system, then going along to a couple of relevant meetings should be beneficial. At all seminars people in one way or another are trying to sell you something, even if (in a members only seminar) it is the benefits to be gained from new technology. But it is seldom a hard sell approach (ie there is hardly ever anyone standing at the exit with order forms) and seminars should be viewed as one of the less intense ways of increasing your knowledge.

EXHIBITIONS

In the early days of the microcomputer exhibition the hall used to be filled with people visiting nearly every stand at the show, and finally leaving with a plastic bag full of brochures and a head full of conflicting advice and recommendations. This was not really to the benefit of the purchaser or the suppliers who had payed a lot of money for their stand. The attitude of business visitors to these exhibitions has now changed to the more sensible one of planning beforehand what you want to see, and then only visiting the stands that are relevant and spending more time on in-depth discussion. This approach is more likely to bring results, and is the one preferred by the suppliers themselves.

The major advantage of these exhibitions is that in the space of one or two days you can visit and talk to a range of suppliers from different locations and discuss what they have to offer and hear their recommendations. It is not really the time and place for a complicated demonstration of a system, but is extremely useful for identifying suppliers that it would be worthwhile talking to in greater detail at a later stage. You may well come across suppliers that you haven't heard of before who can offer just the sort of system that you require.

Exhibitions are also very useful for companies that already have a successful computer installation in place, as they can be used as a sort of 'refresher' course, updating your knowledge of what is happening in the computer marketplace. A number of manufacturers and software houses use exhibitions to launch new products, and it is always useful to learn whether these new items would be of any use to your business. Some people consider that when they get a computer system that that is the end of it for a few years at least, but many of the leading corporations in this country are purchasing new equipment every month, and even if you are not quite in that league it is useful to keep your knowledge of the market up-to-date. A major reason being that these corporations are probably your competitors and it pays to know what they are doing, and computer exhibitions can be very useful sources of competitive information.

CONCLUSION

Seminars, training courses and exhibitions can all be very useful sources of information, and there are a great many to choose from. The trick to effective information gathering is to be selective, to visit only the seminars and exhibitions that are liable to be relevant to the purchase you are considering. For first-time buyers an introductory training course should probably be considered.

The main aim of going to seminars and courses is to increase your level of knowledge, so that when you are faced with a sales executive spouting jargon, or making promises that you find suspicious, *you* can take command of the conversation and endeavour to find out if he or she is offering something worthwhile, or whether they are one of the cowboys. Professional sales executives are delighted to deal with a knowledgeable customer, but cowboys will be frightened away. Visiting these events may at first sight seem a waste of your valuable time, but it will help you to avoid making a costly error, and will help you to recognise a 'con merchant' that much faster.

12 Friends and Acquaintances

A Friend of a Friend has a Computer . . .

GENERAL

In a number of books and magazines you will find the following advice: 'If you are unsure about getting a computer, find out if any of your friends or business acquaintances have one and ask them what their experiences have been. This can often be one of the best sources of guidance.' It this true? Well, yes and no. This is undoubtedly one of the most complex byways of the computer maze, especially when you hear stories like: "My friend bought a computer and from then on everything went wrong. The suppliers were crooks!" Meanwhile the suppliers are saying: "That guy was crazy. He wanted the computer to do absolutely everything, and would only pay tuppence to get it to do it". There are two sides to every story.

Computerisation is now so widespread that nearly everyone who doesn't own one now knows someone who does, or someone who has used one, and everyone has a tale to tell. It is in the nature of these things that it is the horror stories that travel fastest and get the greatest degree of embellishment. The old truism that bad news travels fast certainly holds good in the computer world.

Take the story of Amstrad's new PC as an example. Amstrad had priced it so low that it severely undercut all of the competition. As Amstrad launched their new baby, the potential devastation of the markets really put the frighteners on some of the computer world's biggest companies. Soon interesting rumours began to circulate. "The Amstrad PC has been incorrectly earthed and the whole machine could become live at any moment!" "Amstrad's new PC has burst into flames and melted in someone's test lab!" "ICI has rejected the Amstrad PC for safety reasons." "The Amstrad overheats and distorts the data on the hard disk." "Marks and Spencer, as part of their pre-purchase testing, did a flame test on the Amstrad and it failed." IBM salesmen were talking about the dangers of having a mini-Chernobyl on your desk. These fascinating stories did the rounds of the computer press. But were they true? No.

ICI went to the extent of issuing a public disclaimer of the particular story that involved them, and said they were quite happy to buy Amstrads in certain situations. Even a hard-headed businessman such as Alan Sugar (the owner of Amstrad) admitted that he was surprised and hurt by the dirty tricks operation mounted against his company. The cynics' reaction to that was: "Welcome to the wild world of computer sales, Mr Sugar."

The story above is included to illustrate a central theme about the computer maze: don't believe everything you hear, good or bad. All these stories actually missed the fact that Amstrad did indeed have problems initially. An early batch of machines was manufactured with faulty electrical conductors, and kept cutting out after half an hour's work. Amstrad soon solved that problem, and actually started to sell add-on fan units to kill the rumours of overheating. The only other problem they had was not being able to supply the massive demand for their machines.

This is not to say that talking to friends and acquaintances is not a good idea. It just suggests that you should treat the information you receive with caution. Nothing is ever as simple as black versus white in the maze.

* * *

The best source of advice is from a business in the same industry as yours that has had a great success with their computer purchase. If you have a contact like this it can be a major short-cut to the buying process and enable you to find the right system that much faster. They can point you in the direction of a supplier that knows what they are talking about, and who can supply the right system at the right price. However it pays you not to accept this advice as being totally correct. It is very useful to develop a healthy scepticism about anything you hear, and if the advice turns out to have been accurate, then you will have a pleasant surprise. This is better than ploughing ahead without doing any checks, and only discovering when it is too late that your friend's installation was the exception rather than the rule for that supplier.

At the very least though, advice of this sort is an extremely useful starting point. It lets you know that there is a suitable system available on the market, and even if you are not convinced about the abilities of the supplier, you can then approach other potential suppliers armed with detailed information on the system you require. Suppliers are very happy to be approached by customers who have a clear idea of what they want, because they can tell early on whether it is worth talking to you. Computer suppliers' time is also valuable, and if the potential customer knows precisely what he or she wants, then the time saved benefits them both.

This sort of advice, however, can be very hard to obtain, especially if you are in a highly competitive market. Not only will your competitors be reluctant to tell you about their computer systems, you will probably be reluctant to tell them that you are considering a new purchase. If you are in this position you will just have to seek advice elsewhere.

People sometimes turn to a friend that they consider a computer 'guru' when searching for advice on a new system. This can be very useful in some instances, but these gurus are often people with an academic frame of mind, and although they may indeed know a lot about computing, it can often be the wrong sort of information. They may be experts in the workings of computer systems, but what you need is someone who can relate the systems available on the market to your way of working – a computing analyst with commercial acumen – and someone with a guru mentality is probably not the person to do this. But listen to them all the same, and sift out the pieces of information that are useful to you.

There is also the thorny problem of the 'friendly' computer sales executive. Is he or she really being friendly and helpful, or is it just a sales technique? This is almost impossible to answer, and it depends very much on your ability to judge people. Sometimes business people take it to extremes and consider that all sales people are trying to con them. Others are just too ready to believe everything they are told. As this chapter has attempted to suggest, the more information you have, and the clearer you are about your needs, then the chances of being sold a poor system are greatly reduced. There are a substantial number of sales people who work to a set of professional ethics that should ensure that you get the right system. There is also sound commercial logic in this stance, because if they sell you a good system that their company can fully support, then when you need new equipment you will come back to them. Good professional companies, the type you should be looking for, hire good professional sales people. But beware of 'over-friendly' sales executives, always taking you or your staff out to lunch. They may be genuine, but just watch that they don't attempt to use this friendship to sell you a system you don't really need.

Brief acquaintances telling horror stories can be very damaging to your company's prospects. It is not unknown to hear people say: "We should probably have bought a computer by now, but when you hear all these problems that people have had . . ." Be as sceptical about bad news as you are about good. Some people just like spreading rumours of trouble and strife. Just consider this: all of the UK's leading companies are computerised to varying extents. Many of them have made multiple purchases. Companies that are not computerised are being left behind in the race for increased business and profits.

Computers in themselves do not cause problems – they are merely a management tool to be used (or misused) as you see fit. Utilised correctly they will undoubtedly improve the efficiency and profitability of your business. Even if your business is highly computerised, it is probable that improvements can be made. New improvements in computer technology are announced nearly every week, and whether you like it or not the race to stay ahead of your competitors' computer technology is now a standard part of business life.

Conclusion
Forewarned is Forearmed

GENERAL

As you will have learned from reading this book (if you didn't know already), the computer maze is a complex place. Sales organisations can often be more useful than some 'independent' consultants; 'specialist consultants' are often computer dealers; computer press 'reports' are sometimes no more than rumour mongering. The lines of demarcation within the maze can be very fuzzy – there is a large degree of overlap between certain 'separate' sectors.

The computer maze is an obstacle that you just have to overcome. The maze is that tangle of misdirections that fills the gap between 'knowing you want a computer' and 'knowing what computer to buy'. The main factor that has led some companies down blind alleys, and out wrong exits, is a lack of knowledge. It is seldom as simple as knowing the correct exit. The computer maze usually has to be traversed – and the key to a successful expedition is *knowledge*. The vast majority of computer buyers have too limited a knowledge of what goes on in the maze – the computer world's buying-selling-recommending process. Understanding this process *before* you enter the maze will greatly enhance your prospects of a successful outcome.

The rest of this concluding section outlines some suggestions for a structured approach to gathering this knowledge and putting it to practical use – a structured approach being more likely to give positive results. It is divided into the following sub-sections:

System Requirements Analysis

The first step to take is to analyse your own requirements and to draw up a system specification.

Systems Availability Analysis

Step 2 – do some research into the systems on the market using some of the information sources mentioned earlier.

Supplier Evaluation

Step 3 – find potential suppliers that can meet your requirements specification and evaluate their skills.

The Installation

Too many people think that when they've placed an order the hard work is over, and that can be when disaster strikes – always take Step 4 and plan the installation.

SYSTEM REQUIREMENTS ANALYSIS

The first step to take when planning the purchase of a new computer system is the System Requirements Analysis – analysing your own needs and wants. Too many companies immediately approach potential suppliers with only a very vague idea of what they require. This approach can be very time-consuming (for the supplier as well as the customer), and can easily result in the purchase of an only partially useful system.

The best place to start is with an analysis of what you do now, what procedures you follow, and the outcomes and implications of these procedures. From this analysis you should be able to highlight the problem areas – cashflow inadequacies; stock control problems; information retrieval difficulties, etc.

Once this has been done you can then begin to consider what you would *like* to do in the future. Changes and improvements that would be of benefit should be noted. It pays to be slightly circumspect when considering the future – perfection usually costs a great deal of money and is probably only for those companies with bottomless wallets.

It is usually a good idea at this stage to involve users of your existing system (manual or computerised) and also the potential users of the new system. However good the person or persons are that are set the task of system requirements analysis they may well miss something. Even if the users do not come up with any useful suggestions, at least they will feel they have been consulted, and this may well reduce any potential user resistance to the installation of the new system.

All of this analysis work should be drawn together in a system specification. It is important to stress that this specification should not be considered the final word on the subject, but should be for guidance only. (This should *not* be taken to mean that it can be amended willy-nilly. Major amendments should only occur after detailed re-analysis.) The reason that it is for guidance only is that most prospective purchasers will not be computer experts, and the specification you produce may have implications that you did not consider that may well be clearer to those with computer expertise – for instance there may not be *any* suppliers who can give you exactly what you want. In addition, your potential suppliers may well be able to suggest certain improvements to your existing systems that you hadn't considered. It will probably be well worthwhile for you to listen to these suggestions with an open mind, and not insisting in sticking rigidly to your original specification come what may. The very act of producing this specification will also have the useful effect of concentrating and clarifying your current situation in the minds of those who will be involved in the decision making process.

This specification will also be extremely useful in cutting down the time taken to evaluate potential suppliers. By showing them the specification you have drawn up they can see whether they are capable of supplying the system you desire, which can cut down on a lot of wasted time on both sides, and if they are capable, then it can substantially reduce the amount of time suppliers have to spend in their own analysis of your requirements to make sure that they understand what you want.

There is also the thorny question of who should actually draw up this specification – internal staff or outside consultants. The advantage of using internal staff is that they will have a clear idea of what the present procedures are, and may well have already indentified necessary improvements. You may find that outside consultants spend a substantial proportion of their time in just learning the basics of what you do, and not in proper analysis. Due to the costs involved in using consultants, and the fact that the consultants may lack the necessary knowledge of your business, most companies do the analysis internally – after all you are the people who know your company best.

However there are certain occasions when outside consultancy has positive benefits. One is when the key staff who will be involved in the decision-making process have numerous time constraints, and due to their existing commitments they are unable to allocate the proper amount of time to system requirement analysis. Another is when you and your colleagues feel that you do not have the necessary knowledge of modern technology to arrive at the sort of comprehensive analysis you require. In cases like these outside consultancy should certainly be considered.

The next question is which sort of consultancy organisation to approach. The second part of this book has pointed out that this decision is not as simple as you may have thought. Some independent consultants may lack the necessary knowledge of your type of business, but on the other hand, many of the 'specialist' consultancies may also be computer dealers. One way round this conundrum, if you use a specialist consultant, is to make it absolutely clear that the system specification they produce should be *truly* independent, and not just a write-up of their own system.

From this point you can either, if you have employed a consultant, let them handle the systems and supplier analysis, or if you have produced your own specification (or wish to terminate your contact with the consultant at this point) it is time to look for potential systems and suppliers.

SYSTEMS AVAILABILITY ANALYSIS

Many companies jump straight from producing a systems specification to talking to suppliers. It is better to pause slightly at this stage and to do some research work into the systems available on the market. It is unlikely, though not impossible, that this research will uncover the perfect system for your business, but it is always better to approach potential suppliers with at least a minimum of understanding of just what is on the market.

The key question, of course, is where to look. Part 3 of this book details many of the information sources available to purchasers, and all four chapters have suggestions that can be implemented at this stage. The computer press will keep you up-to-date with latest developments, and the journals that concentrate on particular sectors of the market (such as CAD/CAM) can be very useful. The various directories and guides on the market (such as *The Computer Users' Year Book*, and the NCC's *Computing Decisions*) supply prospective buyers with a very useful overview of present market conditions. But it should always be remembered that these publications are no more than *guides* – they can be out-of-date before they are even published, and they are poor at presenting a comprehensive picture of local computer dealers' strengths (or even their existence). The great strength of these guides is that they can help you to pinpoint software packages that can potentially meet your needs. And the identification of software systems can often lead to the identification of potential hardware suppliers (eg by contacting the software authors and asking for their recommendations).

Books and manuals, often overlooked by companies on the buying trail, may mean a little more work, but their in-depth analysis of current trends can be invaluable to prospective purchasers. Their detailed reviews of current business usage of technology, and their pointers towards successful purchases are probably not available elsewhere. Seminars, courses and exhibitions all contribute to the necessary expansion of a company's knowledge base. And the advice of friends and business acquaintances can often complete (or in some cases distort!) the picture.

This long trawl through numerous journals, and the prospect of visiting a number of potentially boring seminars in the hope of returning with some nuggets of information, may be off-putting to many people. Indeed it may appear unnecessarily time-consuming. But this research work can be amply rewarded when it comes to discussions with potential suppliers. There must be few people who would not feel more comfortable in approaching complex discussions with a sound background knowledge. And this little bit of extra work, leading to some extra knowledge, can make all the difference.

When approaching suppliers remember that this research, like your system specification, is for guidance only. Avoid the trap of becoming convinced that something you've read in the press is the answer to all your problems. This may be true, but it is far safer to carry a healthy scepticism with you in your journey through the computer maze.

SUPPLIER EVALUATION

Having drawn up a system specification, and carried out some research into the systems available, the next step is to identify potential suppliers of your new system. If your research has been particularly fruitful you may already have established the names of some suppliers. This is more likely to be true if your requirements are particularly special, in which case there may be only a few companies capable of installing your system. But in most cases there may be a large number of potential suppliers.

Unless your needs are very specific, the best and most obvious place to start looking is in your local area. If you have already purchased computer equipment in the past (as is the case with most established companies these days) you may already have a fair idea of the skills and targeted market segments of the dealers in your area. But as the computer maze is continually shifting and changing; don't take it for granted that these dealers are still selling exactly the same products. It is more than likely that they have been amending their marketing strategies to suit the new realities of the computer supply world.

If you are unaware of the skill profiles of your local suppliers, then a blanket approach is called for. This usually takes the form of sending out an 'Invitation to Tender'. This is the method that most non-dealer consultancy companies use. This document consists of your system specification, plus any other information you feel is relevant (such as timescale constraints). Although creating such documents can be time-consuming, it is worthwhile making the effort to ensure the ITT is truly comprehensive, as it can avoid a lot of problems later on. It is also important to include a note to the effect that the ITT is not the final word on the subject, otherwise you may exclude some potential suppliers with suggested improvements to your original specification.

The next question is how many ITTs to send out. This is governed by two factors. The first is the complexity of your requirements. If you feel that the system you need is fairly simple and standard, then five or six ITTs are probably sufficient. If it is more complex then a wider spread may be necessary to be able to identify potential suppliers; say, a dozen or more. The second factor is your level of knowledge. If you have a good idea of what type of supplier would be capable of installing your system then you can restrict the mailing list to this group. However if you are unsure about the skills of various suppliers, then send out a larger amount of ITTs.

There are two distinct drawbacks to the ITT method that make it less effective than proper research to identify potential suppliers. The first is that it can be very time-consuming to sift through a number of weighty replies to your specification document. And secondly these replies can often contain conflicting recommendations. It can be a boring task separating the wheat from the chaff. But if your initial research has failed to uncover a list of potential suppliers, then the ITT method may be your only choice.

When you have selected your potential suppliers, your next task is to choose which supplier is the best one to install your new system. This is the 'question' phase. There are a number of standard questions that should always be asked to enable you to establish the supplier's company profile. These questions will cover subjects such as:

The supplier's business turnover

Their existing customer base

Their experience in the market

The type of systems they sell

Their fields of specialisation

This sort of questioning should be supplemented by asking questions that are specific to your requirements, eg have they installed a number of similar systems in the past? And if the answer is no, don't reject them out of hand – ask why they feel confident that they can supply the system you want (they may have an excellent team of programmers).

A key point to realise at this phase is that computer supply is not just about suitable hardware and software; computer dealerships are *people* businesses, and it is the staff that a potential supplier employs that can make all the difference between success and failure. This leads on to a vital conclusion – *always ask questions about the dealer's staff.* For instance, what is their ratio of support people to sales staff; and what are their qualifications (eg if they are selling accounting systems, do they employ any CAs).

This is also an important point when buyers are considering asking for discounts. When you buy a computer system you are not just paying for some hardware and software; you're also paying for the skills that that supplier can offer. So when you see that one supplier can offer you the same system for quite a lot less than another, ask yourself the question why? It may well be that the dealer with the lower price can undercut his competitor precisely because he has not employed qualified and knowledgeable staff – and a lack of proper support could well cost you a lot more money in the long run.

The final part of the Supplier Evaluation phase is to draw your judgements on the supplier's staff. They may well be highly qualified, and display a sound knowledge of your market and your needs – but can you work with them? And, more importantly, do you trust them? The key to a successful installation is two-way communication, and it helps greatly if you can establish a good working relationship from day one.

THE INSTALLATION

Having made your choice of supplier (or suppliers) you are now in a position to install the system. However there are a couple of things that should be fully clarified *before* the physical installation begins. The first, and most important (and too often ignored), is to establish that you and your supplier are in *complete* agreement as to your requirements, and as to what is expected of them (and of you). If this is not done it can lead to unseemly wrangles later on that drag both you and the supplier away from productive work – it is in both your interests to ensure that this agreement is reached. Additionally, don't just rely on a verbal agreement (it was a famous Hollywood producer that said a verbal agreement isn't worth the paper it's written on). Spell it out on paper and get *senior* personnel on both sides to sign it. Taking these fairly simple steps can greatly reduce the potential for hassle later on.

The second important step is to agree on a timetable for the installation. This should not be a one-sided affair with the buyers making all the demands. If you insist on an installation date when the supplier's best support staff are unavailable, then you will be damaging your own interests. The drawing up of this timetable should be done in a spirit of give and take on both sides. Once this timetable is drawn up you should do your best to stick to it. Again if you start trying to amend it later on without proper consultation, you may end up being passed from support person to support person, with the attendant damage that this lack of continuity can wreak.

Due to these potentially grey areas outlined above, it is normally far easier to plan an installation if there is only one supplier involved. Controlling an installation with two or more suppliers can be very complex, but it is a problem that you will just have to overcome if your system requires more than one supplier. The most important point is to clearly establish (in writing!) which supplier is responsible for what, and to make sure that they all agree, and are clear on which are their areas of responsibility.

Another important factor that is vital to a successful installation is user training. The reputation that UK-based companies have for being vastly undertrained compared to our counterparts abroad also tends to hold good even when a new system is being installed. It is amazing how many companies fight tooth and nail to get a few hundred pounds of training costs reduced when they've already spent many thousands on getting the system itself. This is an extremely short-sighted attitude. A computer system is just a tool; a very sophisticated tool, but a tool nonetheless. And like any tool you'll only get your money's worth if you use it properly.

This is particularly true of computers. If they are used incorrectly they can have a seriously detrimental effect on your company's health. They are only worth buying if you are going to use them properly, and the only way you will ever be able to use them properly is if you are fully trained. The moral is quite simple: don't skimp on the training. In most cases cutting down on the amount of training doesn't save you money – it is more liable to cost you money (and a great deal of potential hassle as problems develop among poorly trained users).

Once you have the system installed, give it (and your staff) time to settle in. Don't automatically blame the supplier if things go wrong – the problems may well be due as much to your own staff's inexperience as to anything the supplier has done. Remember that a good working relationship with your supplier will be of major benefit to you when further support is needed. So when problems do occur, pause and analyse the problem to see whom is really at fault before causing unnecessary upsets that may rebound on you later. But if it *is* the supplier's fault, put it down on paper and get it rectified quickly before things get out of hand.

SUMMARY

Taking the steps outlined above may appear time-consuming, but, like many things in life, a successful computer purchase and installation does not come easily. But taking these steps will greatly improve your chances of reaching a successful conclusion, and will repay the effort involved many times over.

The important point to remember is that the obstacles thrown up by the computer maze *can* be overcome, and that armed with your newly gained knowledge you will be suitably sceptical when you see a signpost that says: 'This way to perfection – we've got all the answers.' It may even be true, but ask lots of questions and make the organisation that is making the claim prove it to you. Then use this knowledge practically, by applying it in a structured fashion like that detailed above to find the right exit for you and your company.

* * *

This book is not the end point in a journey – it is the *start* point. In the maze, knowledge is all; and the task of collating and analysing the information you require is entirely up to you. Too many buyers, whether due to time constraints or a lack of understanding of the buying-selling-recommending process, jump straight in to Step 3 – Supplier Evaluation, and generally ignore the information sources outlined in Part 3 of this book.

So buy some magazines, get some directories, and read some books (see the Bibliography at the end of this book for contact addresses) – it will be well worth the effort to you. The right computer system, correctly installed and properly utilised, will make your business more profitable, which is the true reason for buying a system in the first place.

Good luck in your journey through the maze – but effective research and an attainment of a higher level of knowledge will substantially reduce your need to rely on luck!

Appendix 1
Bibliography

This book has stressed the importance of research and the proper utilisation of the information sources available to business buyers. This bibliography has been included to make your access to these sources easier by providing a list of contact addresses for the various books and journals mentioned in the book. This list, like the list of companies named in the book, is for guidance only. It is not an exhaustive listing and is by no means complete, especially when touching on the numerous specialist publications on the market. Like this book as a whole, it should be used as a starting point for your own researches. Have a look at the titles available in your local bookshops to see what other books are on the market, and write to some of the publishers whose names are listed.

The bibliography lists the contact addresses for the publications mentioned in Chapter 9 – The Computer Press, and the books mentioned in Chapter 10 – Books And Manuals.

* * *

The prices in this bibliography (where indicated) are for guidance only: they will almost certainly have changed by the time the present book has been published. Check with the relevant publishers for the latest prices.

JOURNALS FOR THE INEXPERIENCED USER

MICRO DECISION
VNU Business Publications, VNU House, 32–34 Broadwick Street, London W1A 2HG. Tel: 01-439 4242.
£1.25; £14.50 pa.

PC USER
EMAP Business and Computer Publications, 67 Clerkenwell Road, London EC1R 5BH. Tel: 01-430 1200.
£1.75.

PC WEEK
VNU Business Publications (see above)
£161.00 pa.

PERSONAL COMPUTER WORLD
VNU Business Publications (see above).
£1.10; £15.00 pa.

PRACTICAL COMPUTING
Electrical-Electronic Press Limited, Quadrant House, The Quadrant, Sutton, Surrey SM2 5AS. Tel: 01-661 3500.
£1.25; £16.50 pa.

WHAT MICRO?
VNU Business Publications (see above).
£1.00; £12.00 pa.

WHICH COMPUTER?
EMAP Business and Computer Publications (see above).
£1.50; £18.00 pa.

JOURNALS FOR THE EXPERIENCED USER

BYTE
McGraw-Hill Publications Company, 70 Main Street, Peterborough, New Hampshire 03458, USA (but available in some UK bookshops).
£2.50; £46.00 pa.

COMPUTER TALK
Business Press International, Quadrant House, The Quadrant, Sutton, Surrey SM2 5AS. Tel: 01-661 3150.
£18.32 pa.

COMPUTER WEEKLY
Electrical-Electronic Press, Quadrant House, The Quadrant, Sutton, Surrey SM2 5AS. Tel: 01-661 3500.
£40.00 pa.

COMPUTING
VNU Business Publications, VNU House, 32–34 Broadwick Street, London W1A 2HG. Tel: 01-439 4242.
£0.40; £32.00 pa.

MINICOMPUTER NEWS
EMAP Business and Computer Publications, 34 Farringdon Lane, London EC1R 3AU. Tel: 01-251 6222.
£30.00 pa.

PC DEALER
VNU Business Publications (see above).
£55.00 pa.

SPECIALIST JOURNALS

CAD/CAM INTERNATIONAL
EMAP Business and Computer Publications, 67 Clerkenwell Road, London EC1R 5BH. Tel: 01-430 1200.
£24.00 pa.

COMMUNICATIONS MAGAZINE
100 Avenue Road, Swiss Cottage, London NW3 3TP. Tel: 01-935 6611.
£18.00 pa.

COMPUTING DECISIONS
National Computing Centre Limited, Oxford Road, Manchester M1 7ED. Tel: 061-228 6333.
£29.50 pa.

DEC USER
EMAP Business and Computer Publications Limited, 34 Farringdon Lane, London EC1R 3AU. Tel: 01-251 6222.
£18.00 pa.

IBM COMPUTER TODAY
Electrical-Electronic Press, Quadrant House, The Quadrant, Sutton, Surrey SM2 5AS. Tel: 01-661 3500.
£45.00 pa.

OTHER JOURNALS

Many of today's newspapers, such as *The Times*, *The Guardian* and the *Financial Times*, have specialist computer sections. In addition many trade journals, such as *New Civil Engineer* and the *Journal of the IEE*, have regular reviews of new computing developments that are directly relevant to their readers. Many other standard office equipment journals have also substantially increased their coverage of computer-related topics, eg *Office Equipment News*, from AGB Business Publications Limited, Audit House, Field End Road, Eastcote, Middlesex HA4 9LT; Tel: 01-868 4499.

DIRECTORIES AND GUIDES

COMMUNICATIONS USERS' YEARBOOK
Manor House Press Limited, 404/406 Holloway Road, London N7 6QA.
£55.00 pa.

THE COMPUTER USERS' YEAR BOOK
VNU Business Publications, VNU House, 32-34 Broadwick Street, London W1A 2HG. Tel: 01-439 4242.

THE DATA COMMS BOOK
VNU Business Publications (see above).
£35.00.

GUIDE TO COMPUTER AIDED ENGINEERING, MANUFACTURING AND CONSTRUCTION SOFTWARE
National Computing Centre Limited, Oxford Road, Manchester M1 7ED. Tel: 061-228 6333.
£39.50.

MICROSYSTEMS SOFTWARE DIRECTORY
National Computing Centre Limited (see above).
£25.00; £180.00 pa.

MICROSYSTEMS TRAINING DIRECTORY
National Computing Centre Limited (see above).
£25.00; £180.00 pa.

OXFORD SURVEY IN INFORMATION TECHNOLOGY
Oxford University Press, Journals Subscription Department,

Walton Street, Oxford OX2 6DP. Tel: (0865) 56767.
£35.00.

THE PC YEAR BOOK
VNU Business Publications, VNU House, 32-34 Broadwick Street, London W1A 2HG. Tel: 01-439 4242.
£35.00.

THE SOFTWARE GUIDE FOR ACCOUNTANTS
VNU Business Publications (see above).
£35.00.

THE SOFTWARE USERS' YEAR BOOK
VNU Business Publications (see above).

WHARTON'S COMPLETE GUIDE TO OFFICE AUTOMATION
Wharton Information Systems, Regal House, London Road, Twickenham, Middlesex TW1 3QS. Tel: 01-891 6197.
£30.00.

MANUALS

GETTING STARTED WITH WORDSTAR
Cambridge University Press, The Edinburgh Building, Shaftesbury Road, Cambridge CB2 2RU.
£9.95.

MANAGEMENT GUIDE TO CHOOSING AND IMPLEMENTING COMPUTER SYSTEMS
National Computing Centre Limited, Oxford Road, Manchester, M1 7ED. Tel: 061-228 6333.
£50.00.

THE UNIX SYSTEMS USER'S HANDBOOK
Prentice-Hall International Limited, 66 Wood Lane End, Hemel Hempstead, Herts HP2 4RG.
£14.75.

USING THE AMSTRAD WORD PROCESSOR
National Computing Centre Limited (see above).
£8.50.

BOOKS

AUTOMATING YOUR OFFICE
National Computing Centre Limited (NCC), Oxford Road, Manchester, M1 7ED. Tel: 061-228 6333.
£12.50.

COMPUTERISATION GUIDELINES
NCC (see above).
£13.50.

CONTROLLING PC ACQUISITION
NCC (see above).
£9.95.

THE INFORMATION WEAPON – WINNING THE CUSTOMERS AND MARKETS WITH TECHNOLOGY
John Wiley & Sons Limited, Baffins Lane, Chichester, West Sussex PO19 1UD. Tel: (0234) 779777.
£27.50.

INFOTRENDS – PROFITING FROM YOUR INFORMATION RESOURCES
John Wiley & Sons Limited (see above).
£22.90.

MANAGEMENT GUIDE TO OFFICE AUTOMATION
NCC (see above).
£65.00.

PROGRAMMING TECHNIQUES AND PRACTICE
NCC (see above).
£14.95.

SSADM MANUAL (2 Volumes)
NCC (see above).
£140.00.

USING COMPUTERS – A MANAGER'S GUIDE
NCC (see above).
£14.75.

Index